Dynasties

ca. 2100–ca. 1600 B.C.	Xia (Hsia)
ca. 1600–1122 B.C.	Shang, or Yin
1122–770 B.C.	Western Zhou (Chou)
770–256 B.C.	Eastern Zhou (Chou)

Spring and Autumn Period 770–476 B.C.
Warring States Period   475–221 B.C.
Han, Zhao (Chao), Wei, Yan (Yen),
  Qi (Ch'i), Chu, Qin (Ch'in)

221–207 B.C.	Qin (Ch'in)
206 B.C.–24 A.D.	Western Han
25–220	Eastern Han
220–280	Period of the Three Kingdoms

Wei (North)   220–265
Shu (Sichuan)   221–263
Wu (South)   222–280

265–316	Western Jin (Chin)
317–420	Eastern Jin (Chin)
386–589	Period of the Southern and Northern Dynasties

Southern Song (Sung) 420–479
Southern Qi (Ch'i)   479–502
Southern Liang   502–557
Southern Chen   557–589
Northern Wei   386–534
Eastern Wei   534–550
Northern Qi (Ch'i)   550–577
Western Wei   535–556
Northern Zhou (Chou) 557–581

581–618	Sui
618–907	Tang
907–979	Period of the Five Dynasties and Ten Kingdoms

Later Liang   907–923
Later Tang   923–936
Later Jin (Chin)   936–946
Later Han   947–950
Later Zhou (Chou) 951–960
Ten Kingdoms   907–979

960–1127	Northern Song (Sung)
1127–1279	Southern Song (Sung)
916–1125	Liao
1115–1234	Jin (Chin)
1271–1368	Yuan, or Mongolian
1368–1644	Ming
1644–1911	Qing, or Manchu (Ch'ing)

Death of the last Qing emperor, 1967

1912–1949	Republic of China
1949	People's Republic of China

CHINA

The publishers wish to thank
Xu Liyi, Deputy Director,
The National Publishing Administration of China,
and Li Huaizhi,
Director and Editor-in-Chief,
Shanghai People's Art Publishing House,
for making this book possible.

CHI

A book by
Jugoslovenska Revija
and the Shanghai People's Art Publishing House

Authors:
Zheng Shifeng
Chu Shaotang
Liu Shuren
Huang Jiemin
Li Tianren
Lu Xinxian
Zhang Tianlin
Chen Youwen

Design by:
Massimo Vignelli

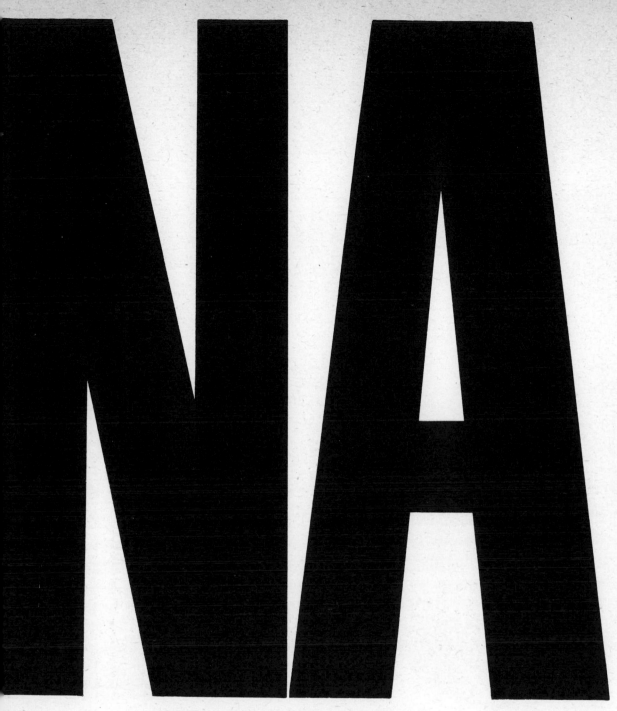

All Provinces and Autonomous Regions

McGraw-Hill Book Company
New York, San Francisco, St. Louis

Library of Congress
Catalog Card Number: 80-23641

First published
in the U.S. and Canada 1980 by
McGraw-Hill Book Co.

ISBN 0-07-056830-8

Director and Editor-in-Chief
Nebojša Tomašević

Edition Editors:
Xu Bingxing
Shen Zaixu
Kosta Rakić

Assistant Editor
Nevenka Mićunović

Translations by:
Lo Chaotien
Yang Zhihong
Sun Liang
Ren Zhiji

Translation Editor
Michael Rose

Production Editor
Miodrag Vartabedijan

Produced by Scala

This book was produced
in cooperation with the
Shanghai People's Art Publishing
House, Shanghai

Director and Editor-in-Chief
Li Huaizhi

Printed and bound
in Milan, Italy by
Amilcare Pizzi Arti Grafiche, SpA
for McGraw-Hill Book Co.
1221 Ave. of the Americas
New York, N.Y. 10020

Photographs by:
Chen Fuli,
Vice President of PAC
Jin Baoyuan*
Yin Fukang*
Chen Chunxuan*
Zhang Hanyi*
Zhang Ying*
Zhang Zulin*
Yang Kelin
Xu Bin
Chen Zaowen
Chen Donglin
E Yi*
Zhang Dongfen*
Yang Minghui*
Ma Mingjun*
Du Yumin*
Wang Guanmin*
Shen Yantai*
Sun Suxian*
Di Xianghua*
Wei Dezhong*
Cukurović Aleksandar
Djordjević Miodrag
Manolev Dimitrije

*Member of PAC,
Photographers Association of China

Cover:
The Sleeping Buddha of Dazu. There are many stone carvings in the county of Dazu, province of Sichuan, among which the biggest are the statues of Buddha on the cliffs of the Baodingshan and Beishan Mountains. This is the eleventh Buddha on the cliffs of Mount Baodingshan, and represents the Buddha passing into Nirvana. Work on the statue, which is 31 m. (102 ft.) long, began in 1175, the second year in the reign of the Emperor Chun Xi of the Southern Song dynasty, and took over seventy years to finish.

A Note on the Spelling of Chinese Words

This book adopts the new system of transliteration of Chinese characters known as Pinyin. This is the system now used by the official news agency of China, Xinhua (Hsinhua), The New York Times, and most other Western newspapers and journals. The system has been adopted by the Chinese and others in an effort to spell words more as they sound when spoken with standard Peking pronunciation.

Some words may thus not be familiar. To help make them more so, we have at appropriate places presented the older spellings, of provinces, seas, and important cities and rivers in parentheses after the new forms—the reader learns, for instance, that the province of Guangdong (Kwantung) has its capital at Gangzhou (Canton). The list of dynasties similarly presents spellings that differ from new ones.

We have not adopted Pinyin without exception. The old spellings of Dr. Sun Yat-sen and Chiang Kai-Shek are retained, for example. But Mao Tse-tung has become Mao Zedong, and Chou En-lai has become Zhou Enlai—and in general we have decisively moved over to the new system.

There is a story that has been handed down in our country for many centuries, the story of Chang E flying to the moon. According to the legend, 4,000 years ago Hou Yi, a powerful tribal chieftain, married a beautiful woman, Chang E, who was possessed by the idea that one day she would be able to reach the moon. When she discovered that her husband had obtained an elixir from the Celestial Queen, Xi Wang Mu, she swallowed the elixir secretly, found that she could fly, and, leaving earth and husband, alighted on the moon, where she lived forever after. For thousands of years this fable has been repeated from generation to generation in China, and whenever Chinese poets wanted to describe the moon in their works, they would bring in some wistful memory of Chang E, alone in her lunar kingdom with only the woodchopper Wu Chang and a little white rabbit for company. In the touching lines of Li Shangyin, the celebrated poet of the Tang dynasty:

Dwelling in the sea of blue sky, with a lonely heart,
Chang E will surely repent of stealing the elixir.

This is a myth, a fairy tale if you like, though like many fairy tales it enshrines a real human desire. And in the end no elixir, but the human magic of science and technology did enable men to put on wings and realize the dream of Chang E. For the first time in history, man has been able to see from another planet the fantastic sight of the earth, his own habitation, traversing the skies like the other heavenly bodies.

The moon, as we now know beyond any doubt, is dead and cold, without atmosphere or palaces, not to speak of Chang E, the woodchopper, or the white rabbit. And yet one curious link with Chang E, still remains. When the astronauts of the twentieth century, standing in her place, looked down on the surface of the earth, only one man-made object was visible to their eyes: the Great Wall of China, 6,400 km. (4,000 mi.) long and over 2,000 years old, a thin line meandering across the map of Asia, reaching back to the days when Chang E was still a reality and human fantasy dwelt in the realm of the imagination rather than among the miracles of modern technological progress.

With a population of more than 950 million and a total area of over 9,500,000 sq. km. (3,700,000 sq. mi.), China is the third largest country in the world, with the longest uninterrupted civilization and the most continuously developing culture in the history of mankind. And China, cut off from the West by formidable geographical barriers, naturally enough assumed from an early time an aura of mystery to Western observers, and became over the centuries an object of ever-increasing curiosity and study for the rest of the civilized world.

Trade routes to China have existed since the earliest days, and we know that in the seventh century, during the Tang dynasty, a delegation was sent to China by its nearest overseas neighbor, Japan. But the most famous of Western visitors in medieval times was Marco Polo, the Venetian traveler who crossed the Pamirs and the Gobi desert and, reaching Dadu (later Beijing, or Peking) in 1274, stayed there for seventeen years in the service of the imperial court of the Mongol Kublai Khan. The account of his experiences which he dictated after his return to Venice in 1295 is by far the most important first-hand record we possess of life in China and other countries of Central Asia at this period. About three centuries later another Italian, Matteo Ricci, followed in the wake of Marco Polo. Ricci, a missionary, was the first to introduce the scientific knowledge of the West into China—particularly in astronomy, geography, mathematics, and medicine—and his books made a valuable contribution to the exchange of ideas between China and Europe. Among his disciples was the Chinese scientist Hsu Guangqi (1562–1633), in whose memory an observatory was set up in Shanghai which remains in operation to this day.

Among recent visitors to China, two of the most warmly remembered are the American writer Edgar Snow and the Canadian doctor Norman Bethune. Both Snow and Bethune came to our country during the thirties of the present century, at a time when the armed forces of the Chinese people were relatively weak and in a difficult situation. In his Book *Red Star over China* Snow produced a piece of unbiased reporting which not only recounted the tremendous epic of the Long March of 1934 but presented the world with a truthful picture of revolutionary China at a time when Western feelings on the subject were both mixed and misinformed. Bethune, who was in China during the long war of resistance to the Japanese invasion, worked tirelessly on the battlefield, tending the wounded and dying. He gave his own life in the end, extolled by Mao Zedong as "an example of absolute selflessness and utter devotion to others."

Nor was this traffic with the outer world a one-way affair. China itself has long felt the need for contact with its neighbors, and as early as the second century A.D. the Chinese were already dispatching trade caravans to Europe via Central Asia, making economic contact with various countries along the famous Silk Road which reached as far afield as Rome and Mali. In the seventh century the itinerant Buddhist abbot Xuan Zhuang (602–664) made a journey along the Ganges and into southern India—an adventurous undertaking which later served as the subject matter for the mythological novel *Traveling Westward*. In this version Xuan Zhuang, accompanied by three disciples possessed of magic powers, vanquishes all kinds of devils and demons and survives a succession of calamities to arrive at last in the Buddhist Paradise of the Western Heaven and eventually to return home bearing authentic Buddhist scriptures. A few decades after Xuan Zhuang's death another eminent Buddhist monk, Jian Zhen (688–763), turned his attention eastward to Japan. He tried six times to embark on the voyage but failed each time owing to bad weather and violent storms; though old and blind, he stuck to his purpose and on the seventh attempt reached his destination, where he became the founder of a Buddhist sect of strict asceticism. Another great seafaring exploit came in the Ming dynasty at the beginning of the fifteenth century, when a series of Chinese merchant fleets under the command of a high-ranking eunuch, Zheng He, made no less than seven crossings of the "Western Ocean," reaching as far as East Africa and the mouth of the Red Sea. Preceding by several decades the voyages of

Columbus, Magellan, and Vasco da Gama, these expeditions rank high in importance in the story of early maritime exploration.

Nevertheless, as far as Europe and the Western world were concerned, it is true to say that China remained for many centuries the country that nobody knew. In the nineteenth century, with improving communications and the growth of Western colonial ambitions, infiltration into China began to increase; after the outbreak of the Opium War in 1840 Western powers invaded or infiltrated China one after another, and as a result a mass of foreigners, of varied backgrounds and nationalities, swarmed into the country as soldiers, missionaries, traders, speculators, and so on. All saw a part of China. For some it was "a slumbering lion," for some "the invalid of East Asia," for others simply "a paradise for adventurers." But for all, or nearly all, the whole remained a puzzle.

China is so vast, so varied, and so old that it cannot be easily understood. The key to present-day China lies in its past, but it is really difficult for an outsider to bring together the necessary comprehension of written records, historical remains, geographical features, natural resources, and social customs, as well as the political, economic, and cultural developments of a society that has been evolving for more than 3,000 years. No wonder that the ancient aura of mystery still lingers on.

Yet, as Zhou Enlai said during an interview with a distinguished foreign guest in 1971, there's nothing mysterious about it. China is no myth, and it is the aim of this book to make some contribution toward dispelling the mystery. Clearly, the book cannot do everything. But what it can do and does do is give a broad, general view of China today, by providing a really comprehensive collection of color pictures of our country, taken for the first time in all its many provinces, by people who love it, live in it, and have made it what it is. Those who have been to China already will find here much to remind them of the beauties they have seen; people who don't know the country at all may find themselves astonished at the variety and grandeur of the scenery, the splendor of China's ancient monuments, and the fascination of its daily life. You may well feel, as you look at these exquisitely poetic photographs, that you will have lived in vain if you do not see the sunrise from the top of Mount Tai, or visit snow-clad Harbin, or float down the lovely Lijiang with its emerald ripples, or see the Great Wall, winding through country where, in the words of Mao Zedong, "the mountains dance like silver snakes and the highlands charge like wax-hued elephants." This book, we hope, may provide for those who want it a golden key with which to open a window onto our country.

Nevertheless, a key is only a key, and even the volume of photographs in this book cannot portray the innermost essence of China or cover all the facets of its crowded life and history. No photographer could do this for you, even if he were a genius. And so perhaps we should preface our tour of the Chinese provinces with a few words about the past and present of China as a whole.

China is large—5,500 km. (3,400 mi.) from the furthest north to furthest south, 5,000 km. (3,100 mi.) from east to west, with a coastline of 18,000 km. (11,300 mi.) and a land boundary of more than 20,000 km. (12,500 mi.). When the sun rises over the eastern edge of the country, the people on its western border have only just passed midnight; in the south the summer lasts for more than six months, in the north winter holds sway for as long or longer. Some two-thirds of Chinese territory is made up of mountains and hill country; concentrated mainly in the west, the mountains include some of the highest peaks in the world (Qomolongma Feng, better known to Western readers as Mount Everest, actually stands on the Sino-Nepalese border) and furnish the sources for the great rivers which flow eastward through China to the Pacific: the Changjiang (the Yangtze), the Huanghe (the Yellow River), the Heilongjiang, the Zhujiang, and the Heihe. It is these huge watercourses that have made China's water resources among the richest in the world and have given rise, over the centuries, to the irrigation systems with which the Chinese people have nourished and fertilized the valleys and plains that lie in the eastern part of their country.

The complex topography of the mountain areas of China not only provides spectacular views of lofty peaks but also produces rich mineral resources beneath the ground. According to data collected so far, the deposits of metal and other minerals in Chinese territory occupy a position of world importance. In addition, extensive oilfields have been found both in the highlands and in the plains, and immense reserves of oil are located under Chinese territorial waters.

China is a country of extraordinary contrasts. The greater part of it lies across the north temperate and subtropical zones (only quite a small area of South China actually falls within the tropics), but owing to its distribution between the latitudes, the widely varying character of its terrain, and the ever-present influence of the Pacific Ocean, the climate changes dramatically between one part of the country and another. The rainfall in the northeast of the island of Taiwan amounts to over 6,000 mm. (240 in.) a year, that in the boundless deserts of Xinjiang is not more than 200 (8 in.). Because of this diversity of conditions, nature has painted a fascinating and colorful picture across this spacious land of ours. South China and the plains of Taiwan are covered with a luxuriant profusion of the evergreen plants typical of the tropics, while in the northeast a dense growth of larches and Korean pines spreads across the slopes of the Greater Xingan Mountains. The rolling grasslands of Inner Mongolia and Gansu, where "the cattle and sheep emerge and disappear as the grass bends in the wind," the desolate highlands of the north and west, and the towering summits of Xizang (Tibet)—all these contrast fantastically with the lush valleys and rich cultivation of the eastern plains and the myriad exotic blooms of the south. In Kunming, in the province of Yunnan, it is spring all the year round, the Xishuang Banna district a natural zoological and botanical garden of a kind hardly to be found anywhere else on earth. On this wondrous, fertile land the ancestors of the Chinese people, from time immemorial, have applied themselves to the painstaking work of taming nature. A million years ago our remote ancestors were already active in the north and southwest regions of present-day China: in 1929 the skull of an ape-man was discovered at Zhoukoudian, near Beijing, and later five more were unearthed on the same spot, as well as quantities of early stone tools, burned bones, and the fossils of over a hundred different animals. More recently bows and arrows, articles of pottery, and fine stone implements some 6,000 years old have been discovered at Banpo, in the province of Shaanxi, and also on the site of an ancient village of Yangshao in the province of Henan. But more important than any of these for the study of modern Chinese history are the finds made near the town of Anyang, also in Henan: here, at the small village of Xiaotun, archeologists have located the ruins of Yin, the ancient capital of the Shang dynasty, which came to power in about 1,000 B.C. Here is evidence of the end of the primitive era and the beginning of a slave-based society with many of the features of later Chinese civilization. Immense numbers of artifacts have been found among the ruins—tools, weapons, and other crafted objects, as well as the remains of palaces and royal tombs, with spacious pits for burying slaves alive with deceased kings and nobles. (Heaps of the bones of dead slaves are concrete evidence, even today, of this gruesome practice.) Still more significant, perhaps, are the finds of inscriptions on cattle bones and tortoise shells which mark the birth of the written Chinese language.

Fortunately for us today, the outstanding achievements of subsequent Chinese history have been recorded both in words and in the buildings and other cultural relics scattered about the ample theater of Chinese civilization. In the beginning, of course, China was not a unified country, but an undefined area inhabited by the various tribes of the Han people. They fought and conquered one another, the more powerful gradually gaining ascendancy over their weaker neighbors. The Xia tribe is the earliest we know with any certainty to have established some sort of control, and it was from the Xia that the Shang dynasty seized power after some 500 years. Under Shang rule activity became concentrated in the fertile plateaus that surround the middle course of the Huanghe, an area that was always to be central to the Chinese people and can with justice be called the cradle of Chinese civilization. Here many of the techniques of the modern world began to be developed: the smelting and casting of bronze, the production and weaving of silk, and above all the development of that system of writing which has lasted, with many changes and adaptations, to the China of today.

With the decline of Shang power, control passed to the Zhou dynasty—first the western Zhou and then, from 770 B.C., the Eastern Zhou, whose rule is generally divided into two picturesquely named periods: the Spring and Autumn Period and the Warring States Period which followed it. This was an era of rapid economic and social growth. Irrigation and the techniques of agriculture were developed, as well as fiscal administration, a penal code, and interstate diplomacy.

In 513 B.C. the smelting of iron was introduced. As a result, farm tools and other iron implements were made, and ploughing with oxen was introduced. But weapons of warfare could be made too, and under the Eastern Zhou the old centralized slave state began to give way to a feudal society in which a rising landlord class claimed more and more right to authority in its own territory. During the Spring and Autumn Period, historical records show, there were more than 140 small princedoms within the Zhou allegiance.

This was the time of Confucious, who lived from 551 to 479 B.C. and whose philosophy and teachings grew entirely out of the social conditions that surrounded him. Concerned above all to maintain the structure of society in a dangerous period of change, he developed his concept of "righteousness," which required the obedience of son to father, of subject to emperor, and of emperor to heaven. It was essentially a hierarchical and conservative philosophy, well adapted to the needs of a feudal society, and for 2,000 years it exerted a profound influence on the aristocrats, intellectuals, and officials of the Chinese empire; emperors grasped at it in justification and support of an absolute feudal rule that admitted no variation through the centuries, and the governing classes developed its principles into one of the most extensive and rigidly structured bureaucracies the world has ever seen. But it was also essentially antagonistic to new ideas, and to the emergence of disruptive social forces, and much that was backward in China must undoubtedly be attributed to its influence. This is why Confucianism has been attacked in recent times as a philosophy that has hindered the true development of Chinese society over the centuries.

With the proliferation of princelings in the latter part of the Spring and Autumn Period, a struggle for power became inevitable, and reduced itself at least to a conflict between the seven Warring States of Han, Zhao, Wei, Yan, Qi, Chu and Qin. The victory eventually went to the state of Qin, and the Qin leader, Shi Huang, after throwing over the last of the Zhou emperors, imposed his rule on the other states and in 221 B.C. united China for the first time. Though the Qin dynasty did not last long (it was overthrown by a popular uprising after about fifteen years), it gave its name to China—Q in Chinese being pronounced as Ch—and began in earnest the long and complex succession of dynasties that can best be studied in the chronological list at the beginning of this book.

Not all of them ruled over all of China by any means. There were constant shifts of power and authority within the feudal framework, and the brutality and ruthless oppression displayed by most of the rulers resulted in uprisings at regular intervals throughout Chinese history. There were several periods when the empire was split into two, three, or even more subdivisions, with rival dynasties in different areas struggling for ascendancy or coexisting peacefully with their neighbors. And there were invaders from outside—the Mongols, for example, who were not Chinese at all, but established the Yuan dynasty at Beijing for a hundred years in the thirteenth century.

One of the greatest periods in Chinese history began with the reunion of the whole country under the Sui dynasty near the end of the sixth century. The Sui rule lasted for less than forty years, but was replaced by the Tang dynasty, which lasted for nearly 300. Under the Tang Emperors China became one of the most powerful states not only in Asia but in the whole world. The economy developed, trade flourished, and the arts, particularly poetry, reached a high level. And there were more great periods of Chinese achievement in the Song dynasty, which supplanted the Tang after a short interval, and the Ming dynasty of the fourteenth to seventeenth centuries. Chinese history has come down to us as the detailed record of a continuously developing human society. China has seen the growth and the disintegration of the slave state, the formation and consolidation of the feudal system that followed it, and the long decline of that system into a semifeudal, semicolonial regime, more and more subject to foreign exploitation and attack. After the outbreak of the Opium War in 1840, China became the prey, first of the Western powers, then of its own aggressive neighbors, and more than a century passed before it managed finally to rid itself of their influence and, with the victory of the people's revolution, establish the People's Republic of today. China in 1980 is a unified brotherhood of fifty-six nationalities scattered about in different areas of the country. The shackles of age-old serfdom are gone at last. Many ethnic groups, like the Drung, the Nu, the Benglong, and the Jingpo in Yunnan, or the Orogen and the Ewenki in the northeast, or the Li on the island of Hainan, who were lingering at the time of the liberation in the last days of a primitive society, have skipped a thousand years of historical development and stepped straight into modern life. Nevertheless, whatever the harshness and brutality of much of China's past, it must be remembered that the constellation of warring aristocracies who ruled the different nations of our country strove continuously to protect and consolidate it, and that national heroes have emerged throughout its history to fight against invading tribes and uphold national unity. Many, too, were the attempts to bind the country together by more peaceful means: Wang Zhaojun of the Han dynasty, who married the ruler of Mongolia, and the Princess Wen Cheng of the Tang, who became the wife of the ruler of Tibet, were figures symbolic of the desire for closer union between the Han emperors and their neighboring states. Among soldiers Yue Fei, of the Song dynasty, was a typical patriot, resisting the aggression of the Nuzhen aristocrats who founded the Jin dynasty, and in the past hundred years many comparable heroes have arisen to fight with imperialists and feudal rulers. The tombs and shrines of these heroic figures are still intact today: both the Chinese and their foreign visitors pay homage to Yue Fei at his majestic tomb near the West Lake at Hangzhou (Hangchow), that "paradise on earth," and the stately mausoleum of Sun Zhongshan, or Dr. Sun Yat-sen, the great leader who overthrew the last dynasty of China, stands near Nanjing, city of "the crouching tiger and the curling dragon."

In their long struggle with nature the Chinese have amassed a rich stock of experience and have made countless discoveries and inventions in science and technology, many of them at an amazingly early date. It is said that the wheelbarrow, the crossbow, and the kite were originally Chinese inventions. As early as the fifth century B.C., in the *Spring and Autumn* chronicle written by Confucious during the Zhou dynasty, there is a record of a comet that had entered the galaxy in 611 B.C.; at this time the Chinese already knew that a year consists of 365¼ days. As is well known, the magnetic compass was first used in China 2,200 years ago, and in the second century A.D. the eminent astronomer Zhang Heng invented the first seismograph in the world, as well as the armillary sphere, an instrument which can quite accurately determine the location and movement of the heavenly bodies. In the fifth century the mathematician Zu Chongzhi, calculating the ratio between the circumference of a circle and its diameter, worked out the precise figure of π as between 3.1415926 and 3.1415927. Paper was already being produced in China in the second century A.D., and in the seventh century printing from type was invented. In the tenth century the Chinese began to make rockets with niter powder, and at the beginning of the eleventh gunpowder was employed in firing. The list is endless, and even though the conditions of Chinese feudal society did not always allow the proper development of these scientific achievements, they remain an impressive testimony to Chinese ingenuity and skill through the centuries.

In the realms of the humanities and the fine arts, the masters of art and literature have left us a wonderful heritage. The early anthology known as *The Book of Poetry,* a collection of folk songs and ballads with a number of lyrics and other poems by nobles, officials, and men of letters, was compiled by Confucious in the Spring and Autumn Period; but the first major poet of China was Qu Yuan (343–278 B.C.), a native of the state of Chu during the Warring States Period, whose works are collected in the *Poems of Chu.* His masterpiece, the long poem *Li Sao (Sorrowful Complaint),* has enjoyed wide circulation both in China and abroad. The *Yue Fu* of the Han dynasty are again folk songs and popular ballads, collected by an imperial conservatory, and the *Fu* of the same period are a kind of descriptive prose interspersed with verse; but with the Tang dynasty we meet two poets of international reputation, Li Bai (Li Po) and Du Fu. The Yuan dynasty was famous particularly for its drama. Guan Hanqing (ca. 1210–1300), whose masterpiece is the play *The Tragedy of Dou E,* may in certain respects be likened to Shakespeare, and his plays were appreciated by Goethe and Voltaire. *A Story of the West Chamber,* by the other great Yuan playwright, Wang Shifu, has been performed in London and other Western cities during the present century. In the Ming and Qing dynasties the novel became an important literary form, perhaps best represented both inside and outside China by *A Dream of Red Mansions,* the most famous work of the Qing novelist Cao Xuejin.

The Chinese talent for the plastic arts is something which has long been known the world over, and which can be glimpsed in the pages of this book. Any visitor to our country must marvel at the exquisite clay figurines and fine utensils made by our ancestors 3,000 years ago and now unearthed at the village of Yangshao in the province of Henan. If you look at the frescoes in the Dunhaung caves, which date from 366 A.D., or examine the thousands of Buddhist statues and sculptures carved in the Yunggang and Longmeng grottoes, or if you walk round the Taihe Dian (the Hall of Supreme Harmony) and the Temple of Heaven in Beijing, how can you fail to be astonished by these masterpieces that belong among the highest cultural achievements of mankind? As for the subtle, miraculous products of Chinese porcelain, these have already gained so high a reputation in the outside world that comment here seems almost superfluous. How is it, then, that a culture so strong and so varied failed to impose itself with greater effect on the world outside? The answer lies in the paralyzing grip exercised by the feudal and dynastic system that dominated China for almost all of the last 2,000 years. In the end the very rigidity of this system promoted its own decline, resulting in the decadent traditionalism that had no strength left to oppose the imperialistic ambitions of the nineteenth century. With the Opium War the Western powers declared their intentions, and a decade later the answer came with the Taiping Rebellion, the most important peasant revolt in Chinese history, when Hong Xiuquan and his followers attempted to establish a "heavenly kingdom of great peace" in defiance of both foreign influence and the dynastic government of China. The Taiping "heavenly kingdom" lasted until 1864, when it was finally suppressed by the Manchu dynasty in Beijing, with the aid of French and British troops, and foreign influence seemed to be restored. Nevertheless, the formation of the Tung Meng Hui Society (later the Kuomintang) by Dr. Sun Yat-sen in 1895 and the Boxer Rising, which attempted, unsuccessfully, to expel foreigners in 1900, were straws in the wind. Thousands of tons of gold and silver had been shipped to the West, and the imperialist powers had been enriched by cheap "coolie" labor. The sense of revolt was growing, and in 1911, with the democratic revolution led by Sun Yat-sen, the five-colored flag of "the five nationalities supporting the republic" finally replaced the dragon banner of the Qing dynasty.

The last feudal dynasty had been toppled, but that did not mean victory for the Chinese Revolution. The people had yet to suffer many setbacks and failures before they seized political power. Over a period of twenty-eight years, under the leadership of the Communist Party of China, established in 1921, the Chinese people carried on a bitter struggle and overcame innumerable hardships before they won the final victory of the Revolution. The Long March of 1934 is one of the great epics of modern history. With poor equipment and scanty supplies, the Chinese Red Army was surrounded and pursued by Kuomintang troops much superior to it in number. Nevertheless, the army managed to get across from the eastern part of China to the southwest, and thence marched northward. Wearing straw sandals, the guerrillas trekked across desolate grasslands and climbed over snow-capped mountains covering 12,500 km. (7,800 mi.) in a total of 368 days. They endured unimaginable sufferings, hunger, and exhaustion but kept on, thus kindling the flame of hope for the whole nation.

On October 1, 1949, at the historic moment when the five-starred Red Flag was first unfolded over Tienanmen Square, Mao Zedong declared to the world the founding of the People's Republic of China. Only then did the Chinese people reach the end of a path of suffering trodden for thousands of years and stand as a liberated nation. Then did the history of China turn over a new leaf.

Old China used to be called "the invalid of East Asia" or "a heap of loose sand." However, under the leadership of the Communist Party of China and the people's government, the Chinese people have defeated enemies at home and abroad, promoted the socialist revolution, and built up an independent and complete system of industry and national economy. The peasants who form 80% of the total population, have joined the people's communes in a typically Chinese style of big collective agriculture. The national output of grain in 1978 is 1.7 times as much as that in 1949. The means of transportation have also developed rapidly: there are railways from Beijing to every province and administrative area except Xizang, some of them built through precipitous mountains. In science and technology, China is exerting every effort to change its present state of backwardness, and has achieved much even in such advanced spheres as space research and nuclear physics.

The way of progress is never smooth. During the ten years from 1966 to 1976 the process of reconstruction in China suffered serious setbacks owing to the activities of Lin Biao and "the Gang of Four." They were vanquished at the end. At present, under the leadership of the Chinese Communist Party headed by Hua Guofeng, the Chinese people are going ahead toward the goal of "four modernizations"—industry, agriculture, science, and national defense. Today the Chinese are engaged in a work more difficult than the building of the Great Wall 2,000 years ago: to help ourselves (one-fourth of the world's population) progress from poverty to wealth, so that China may become a powerful pillar of peace and stability having an important impact on the future of mankind.

This book presents a true picture of China at the beginning of the eighties. China is still a developing socialist country. In comparison with the old society thirty years ago, many features have changed, but China is still poor and backward in comparison with the advanced nations. Its people, however, will keep on transforming their country and improving its condition. In the river of history 3,000 years are of little account. But as an ancient Chinese saying goes, "Innumerable changes take place in the twinkling of an eye," and perhaps this comment may never have been more apt for China than it is today.

1. *Fireworks, a Chinese invention, have always played an important part in civil life, many celebrations being marked by elaborate and ingenious displays. This ancient tradition is maintained to mark Revolution Day in Beijing.*

2. *Of the mountains that cover three-quarters of China, those of the subtropical Guilin region are among the most beautiful and unusual. For centuries their thrusting peaks, reflected in lakes and rivers, have inspired painters and poets.*

3. *Bathing Horses (detail) by Zhao Mengfu (1254-1322) of the Yuan dynasty (painted on silk). Both the subject and technique are common in Chinese art.*

4. *Colourful, ornate lanterns are a prominent decorative feature of Chinese interiors.*

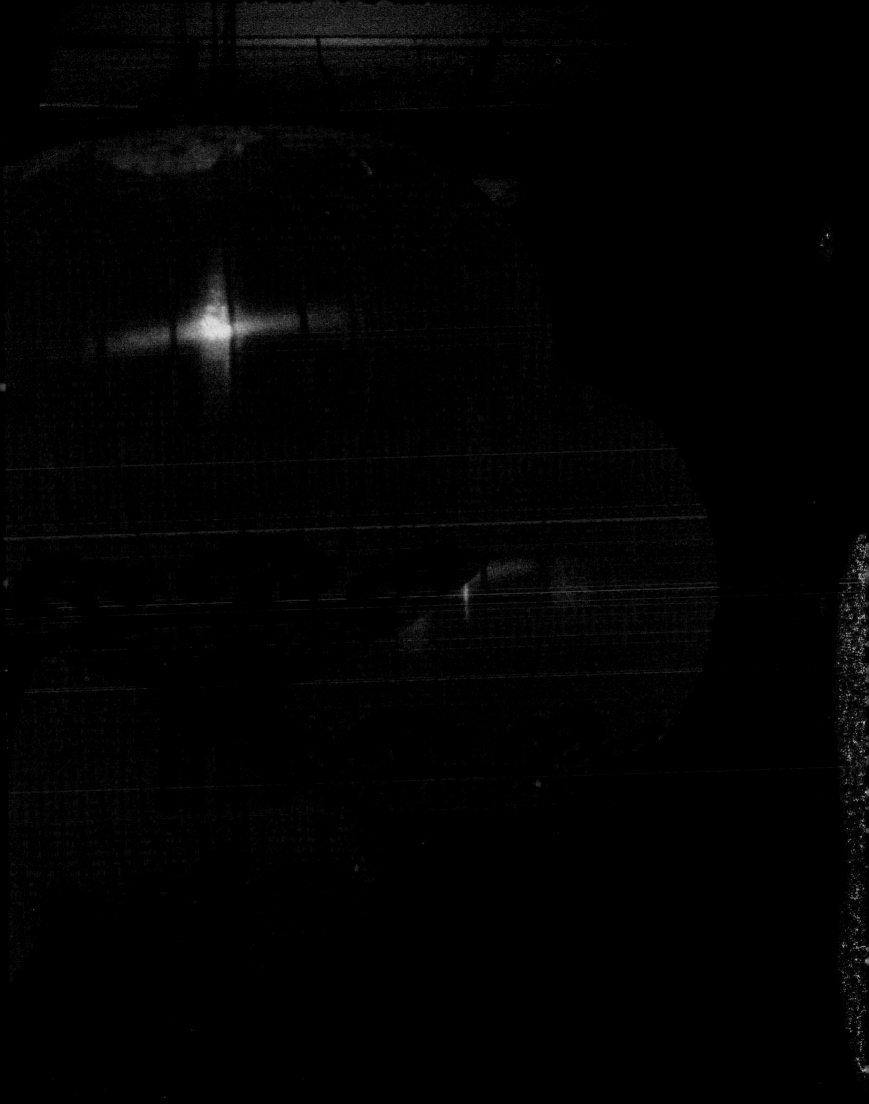

Chapter 1 Beijing

1. The city through the ages

2. Peking Man

3. The Forbidden City—the Imperial Palace

4. The Ming Tombs

5. The splendor of an ancient culture

6. The capital today

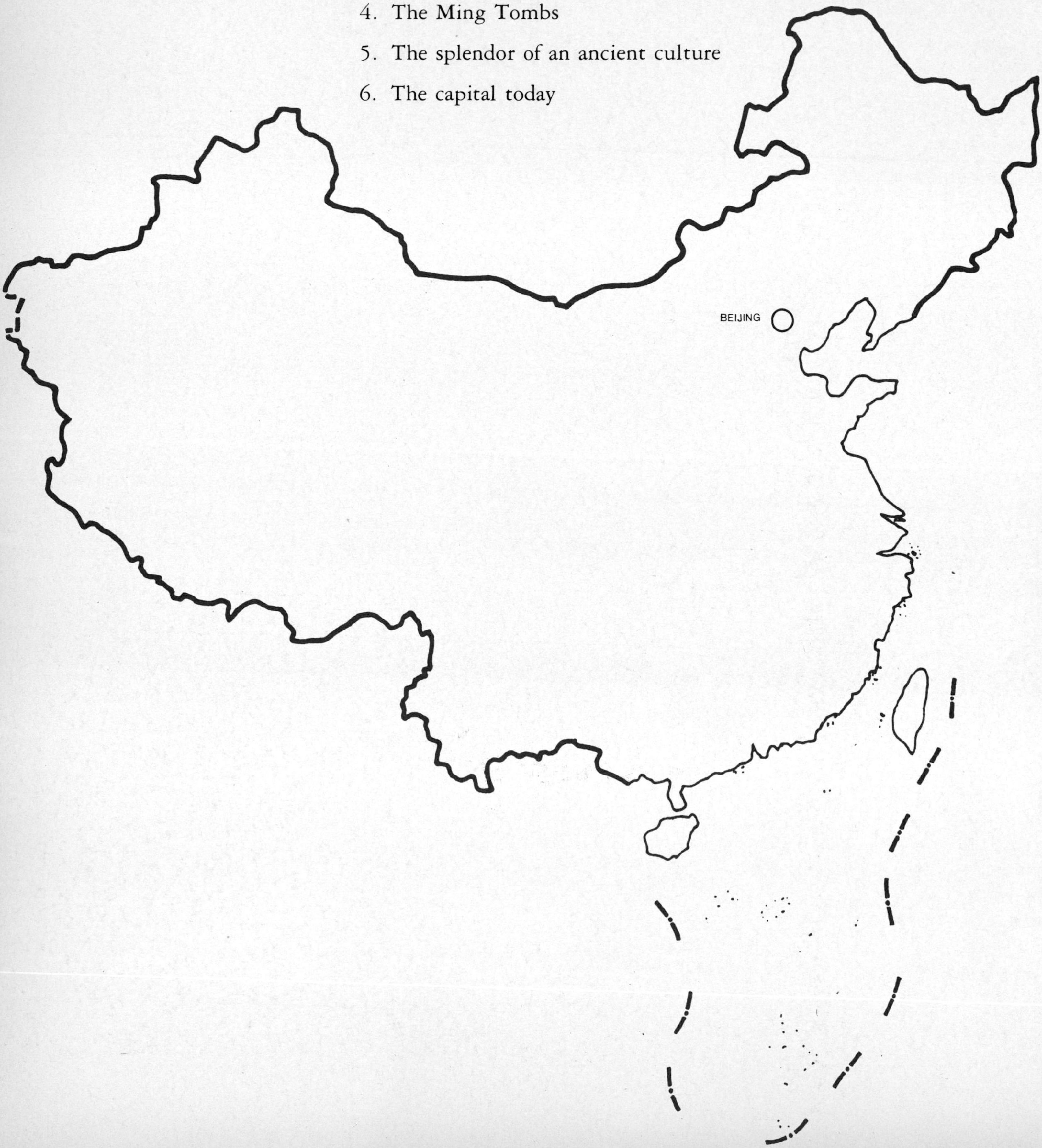

BEIJING ◯

Beijing, better known to Westerners as Peking, is situated about 140 km. (88 mi.) from the coast of the Bohai Sea (Gulf of Po Hai), in the region of North China. Since October 1, 1949, it has been the capital of the People's Republic of China, and it is the political, scientific, and cultural center of the whole country. The city is divided into nine districts and nine suburban counties, with a total area of nearly 18,000 sq. km. (7,000 sq. mi.) and a population of around 8 million.

1. The city through the ages

Beijing has a long history. "Peking Man," whose skull was unearthed here in 1929, dates back some half a million years, and the Great Wall of China, built more than 2,000 years ago and one of the architectural wonders of the world, passes a few kilometers from the city on its way westward. Beijing, under various names, has been the capital of five successive imperial dynasties as well as two republics, and still preserves intact the ancient imperial city with its royal temples and palaces, where every brick, tile, and piece of wood bears witness to a historic past.

About 2,300 years ago, during the Period of the Warring States, Beijing (then called Ji City) was the capital of the slave-owning state of Yan. With the unification of the seven states under the Qin dynasty the capital of China passed elsewhere, and it was not until the beginning of the tenth century that Ji City fell into the hands of the Qidan people from the northeast and, renamed Yanjin, became one of the capitals of the Liao dynasty. Under the succeeding Jin dynasty, early in the twelfth century, Yanjin was rebuilt on a grander scale and given the new name of Zhongdu, only to fall, in 1215, to the invincible horsemen of the great Mongolian leader Genghis Khan. It was Genghis Khan's grandson Hubilie (Kublai Khan), the founder of the Yuan dynasty, who rebuilt it yet again, as the city of Dadu, in the magnificent style which Marco Polo described in such glowing terms to an unbelieving Western world.

A hundred years after the reconstruction, the Han leader Zhou Yuanzhang inaugurated the Ming dynasty with Nanjing (Nanking) as its capital, but after his death in 1398 his son Zhou Di moved the imperial residence back again to Dadu, which now became Beiping and finally, in 1403, Beijing. That is the origin of the name and also, to a great extent, the origin of the present city. For Zhou Di once again transformed the city's appearance, building palaces and temples on a vast scale and so providing it with the architectural splendors which it has retained through the years of the succeeding Qing dynasty into the present day.

After the revolution of 1911, led by Sun Yatsen, Beijing became the center of activity against the northern feudal warlords. It was here that the May 4 Movement began on May 4, 1919—the anti-imperialist revolutionary movement which marked the turning point between the old and the new democratic revolutions in China. Here too, on December 9, 1935, occurred the large-scale outbreak of the students' patriotic movement, which served as a psychological preparation for the later Japanese war. It was in Beijing that the activist writer Lu Xun carried on his revolutionary struggle; it was here also that the early Chinese Communist Li Dazhao went to the gallows. Then in 1948, when the Chinese People's Liberation Army had encircled the city, Beijing was peacefully liberated after many years of strife.

2. Peking Man

Half a century ago, on December 2, 1929, a young Chinese anthropologist, Bei Wenzhong, unearthed the skull of an ape-man 500,000 years old from the limestone formations of Longgushan, in the area of Zhoukoudian only 50 km. (31 mi.) from Beijing. The discovery aroused tremendous interest among anthropologists all over the world, and subsequently six more complete skulls, as well as bones, teeth, and other fragments, were dug out of the soft rock.

The home of "Peking Man" was a cavern, 140 m. (460 ft.) in length. The floor was covered with heaps of debris and layer on layer of fossils, more than 40 m. (130 ft.) thick—a record of the lives of generations of ape-men over a period of 300,000 years and a treasure house of scientific research material and prehistoric information. At the summit of the cavern was a chamber which became known as the Peak Grotto, occupied 18,000 years ago by "Peak Grotto Man," an earlier stage of real human being. This fellow looked much like his counterpart today, and knew how to use implements, make fires, and wear ornaments. So it is clear that the early ancestors of mankind lived, labored, and raised their families in the area around the present-day capital of China.

3. The Forbidden City—the Imperial Palace

The last of the Chinese emperors, Emperor Pu Yi of the Qing dynasty, was born in 1906 and came to the throne at the age of five; he was deposed by the revolution of 1911 and imprisoned in the Imperial Palace, where he lived out the remainder of his childhood in strange isolation. In his book *From Emperor to Citizen* he gave a detailed description of his existence in these early years, and it is curious today to be able to see many of the places and objects which he described still preserved intact in the Imperial Palace Museum.

The Imperial Palace was long known as the Forbidden City, for this was the seat of the emperor and the imperial court, and it was strictly forbidden for anyone outside the court or the government even to approach the gates. Built more than 500 years ago by the first emperors of the Ming dynasty, it is a vast complex of buildings containing more than 9,000 halls and smaller rooms, and it constitutes the most complete of the royal palaces as well as the largest group of ancient buildings in China. It covers an area of 720,000 sq. m. (178 acres), and is surrounded by a wall 10 m. (33 ft.) high and a moat more than 50 m. (165 ft.) wide. Three hundred thousand workmen—famous artisans, civilians, and soldiers—were pressed into its construction over a period of fifteen years, and on its completion twenty-four successive emperors of the Ming and Qing dynasties lived in it, leading lives of luxury and absolute power. For the Ming dynasty alone there are records of 9,000 imperial maids of honor and 100,000 eunuchs. The Imperial Palace may be roughly divided into the outer court and the inner court. Taihe Dian (the Hall of Supreme Harmony), Zhonghe Dian (the Hall of Perfect Harmony) and Baohe Dian (the Hall for the Preservation of Harmony) form the center of the outer court. From Taihe Dian, the emperor's audience hall, the ruler of China issued his edicts, announced his lists of appointments, and sent out generals to command his expeditionary forces. In Zhonghe Dian he rested from his labors, and in Baohe Dian, the banqueting hall, he feasted with his courtiers and guests. The two wings connecting these three halls, Wenhua Dian (the Palace of Civil Virtues) and Wuyin Dian (the Palace of Military Prowess), were used for the discussion of affairs of state with ministers and for other conferences with military and literary attendants. When the peasant uprising under Li Zichan captured Beijing in 1644, it was in Wuyin Dian that the triumphant leader set up his peasant government.

The center of the inner court consists of Qianqing Gong (the Palace of Heavenly Purity), Jiaotai Dian (the Hall of Union), and Kuongning Gong (the Palace of Earthly Tranquility). The emperor lived in Qianqing Gong, the empress lived in Kuongning Gong (where the "warm in winter" chamber was the emperor's bridal chamber), and the maids of honor were housed in the east and west wings facing the imperial gardens to the north. On the eve of Li Zichan's entry into Beijing in 1644, the last emperor of the Ming dynasty, Zhou Youjian, killed with his own hands the maids of honor and his own daughter and hanged himself behind the palace on Coal Hill, now called Jingshan. Today this is a park open to the public, where the ordinary people of Peking can walk at their ease in the Forbidden City and remember the story of the feudal emperor who went to his death here more than 300 years ago.

4. The Ming Tombs

The Chinese feudal emperors lived in luxury and splendor during their lifetimes, and in their old age built themselves grandiose, impregnable tombs in which to end their earthly existence. But they did not end it alone, preferring to take with them a company of maids of honor chosen from among those who happened to be in the imperial household at the time of the emperor's death. This gruesome custom, apparently considered (at least by those who didn't have to take part in it) as a sort of twisted honor, continued right up to the Ming dynasty in the fifteenth century: in the Long Tomb of the Ming dynasty alone more than thirty maids of honor were buried alive.

The Ming Tombs, also called the Thirteen Tombs, are about 50 km. (31 mi.) from Beijing. They were built between 300 and 500 years ago, and are spread out over an area some 40 km. (25 mi.) wide. The great avenue

leading from the central gate is flanked on either side by eighteen pairs of scrupulously carved giant figures of human beings and animals, and the tombs themselves are nothing like the simple burial chambers with which the word is normally associated, but are vast burial palaces, only partly subterranean, designed to reflect the glory of their imperial tenants during their lives.

The Long Tomb, the largest of all, was the burial place of the Emperor Zhou Di of the Ming dynasty. It consists of three courts. The main building is the Sacrificial Hall, consisting of nine chambers, all high and spacious, with a total area of almost 2,000 sq. m. (22,000 sq. ft.). The thirty-two pillars of the main hall are made of whole cedar trunks, the four biggest with a diameter of 1.17 m. (3.9 ft.). Also important are the Yong Tomb and the Ding Tomb, the resting places respectively of the Emperors Zhou Houchong (1507–1566) and Zhou Xijun (1563–1620). Sadly, the Sacrificial Hall of the Yong Tomb was destroyed in wartime, and that of the Ding Tomb burned down in 1914, so that now only parts of the remains can be seen.

Every one of the Thirteen Tombs has a subterranean palace containing the coffins of the emperor and the empress and a great deal of precious jewelry. So far, only the subterranean palace of the Ding Tomb has been excavated since the Revolution. This consists of five halls with a total area of 1,195 sq. m. (13,265 sq. ft.), and contains large numbers of utensils made of gold, silver, jade, and porcelain, as well as silk garments and two precious crowns; the Dragon Crown of the emperor and the Phoenix Crown of the empress, both made of gold thread.

5. The splendor of an ancient culture

The long history of China has given rise to a typically Chinese style in culture and art, within which each dynasty has produced its own characteristic variations. The great playwright Wang Shifu of the Yuan dynasty, some seven hundred years ago, was a native of Beijing; his play *Chronicles of the Western Chamber,* one of the most outstanding Chinese literary works, reached the outer world in the eighteenth century. The most remarkable piece of work in the history of Chinese literature, however, is the great realistic novel *Dreams of the Red Mansion.* Its author, Cao Xueqin, was born in the early eighteenth century, and his whole life was inseparably connected with Beijing. To turn to another art, the great singer of the Peking Opera, Mei Lan-fan, well known all over the world, studied in Beijing and later settled down there. The fifty years of his stage career marked a brilliant chapter in the history of the Chinese dramatic arts. The modern Chinese literary giant Lu Xun lived and worked in Beijing. His home has now become the Lu Xun Museum, where everything is preserved exactly as it was during his lifetime.

The ancient city that has seen so many dynasties has also left us a precious inheritance of architectural monuments. Besides the Imperial Palace, the most interesting are the Beihai Park, the Temple of Heaven, the Summer Palace, and the Great Wall.

The Beihai Park, by the side of the Imperial Palace, was originally a part of the palace of the emperors of the Liao and Jin dynasties, and later an imperial garden. Its origins reach right back into ancient Chinese mythology. According to tradition, there used to be three islands in the North China Sea inhabited by fairies who lived in sumptuous palaces forever. As far back as 320 B.C. one of the rulers of the state of Qi sent out emissaries to the islands in search of the herbs believed to be there which would give everlasting life, and later the first emperor of the Qin dynasty tried again, sending out Xu Fu with 500 virgin boys and girls, none of whom came back. In 104 B.C. the Emperor Wu of the Han dynasty, though he did not repeat this silly business, still could not get the affair out of his mind, so he had a lake dug out and hills heaped up behind the Imperial Palace to symbolize the fairyland. Later emperors followed his example and made additions to Beihai, so that in the end it grew into a park with a large lake and hills as well as rows of palaces and pavilions, a spectacular "fairyland on earth."

The Dagoba (that is, pagoda in Tibetan style) in Beihai Park was built in 1651; it is 35.9 m. (118.5 ft.) in height, and from it the panorama of the whole city of Beijing comes into view. Also in the park is the Nine Dragon Screen in mosaic, built with glazed bricks, with nine curling multicolored dragons on each side. On the north bank of the lake are various beauty spots such as the Little West Heaven, the monument in glazed tiles, the Wall with Iron Shadows, and the Pavilion with Five Dragons. Opposite the Dagoba is the Round City, a palatial building erected in the twelfth century. In the Chenuang Hall there is a Buddha carved from a single piece of unspotted white jade, 1.5 m. (5 ft.) in height. There is also a jar carved from a single piece of black jade. According to tradition, in the thirteenth-century Emperor Hubilie (Kublai Khan) gave a banquet to his high officials and used the jar as a wine container.

The Temple of Heaven lies to the south of Beijing. Like the Imperial Palace, it is a product of the early days of the Ming dynasty. There the emperors of the Ming and Qing dynasties made sacrifices to heaven and prayed for good harvests. The main building, called the Hall of Prayer for Good Harvest, is a triumph of architectural ingenuity and style. It is a circular chamber with three tiers of eaves and a gilded roof, with blue glazed tiles used to symbolize heaven. The whole structure stands on a three-tiered marble base measuring 5,900 sq. m. (1.5 acres), and is supported by wooden pillars, the innermost four symbolizing the four seasons of the year, the middle twelve the twelve months of the year, and the outer twelve the traditional Chinese twelve two-hour periods. At the center of the temple is a round stone with natural designs on it that give the impression of a dragon and a phoenix. The dome of the temple is 19.5 m. (64.4 ft.) high with a diameter of 15.6 m. (51.5 ft.), but there are no internal pillars—only three layers of scaffoldings on the principle of an umbrella (the bottom layer being the longest, the top layer the shortest). This kind of architectural design is rare in ancient times. The round altar has three tiers of marble, with two walls, the outer one being square and the inner one round. The number of stone slates of the altar, the steps, and the balustrade are either nine or multiples of nine, so that they form a complete geometrical pattern. If you stand at the center of the altar and speak, your voice sounds loud to yourself but not to others—a reversal of the more usual acoustic phenomenon which says something interesting about Chinese religious experience, and shows that the Chinese in the Ming dynasty already understood the principle of the reflex of sound waves.

The Summer Palace of Beijing is inseparably connected with the name of one of the most autocratic figures in the recent history of China, for it was here that the Empress Dowager Ci Xi (1835–1908) of the late Qing dynasty wielded the scepter and spent her old age.

As far back as 800 years ago the feudal monarchs had taken a liking for the beautiful scenery around the Summer Palace, and during the Qing dynasty great construction works were carried out and the place was made into the largest garden in China. In 1860, however, British and French troops entered Beijing and the Summer Palace did not escape the ravage. Nothing daunted, the empress dowager set about its reconstruction, using funds that had been set aside for the modernization of the Chinese navy; ironically, the only ship the funds produced was a stone one, designed as a pleasure house on the shores of the Summer Palace's Lake Kun Ming. In 1900 the forces of eight allied powers entered China, and the Summer Palace suffered for a second time, but in 1902 the empress again appropriated funds for its reconstruction. Here this powerful old woman spent her summers, celebrated her birthdays in magnificent style, and watched performances of Peking Opera. Here too she entertained foreign diplomats and other guests, and held under her power her husband, the Emperor Guang Xu, one of the few Chinese rulers who had attempted to introduce political reforms. Today the Summer Palace has been turned into a national park, and what was a paradise for feudal emperors can be enjoyed by the people of Beijing and their many foreign visitors.

To the north of Beijing, at its nearest a mere 50 km. (31 mi.) away, winds the Great Wall of China, the vast rampart built over 2,000 years ago to protect the northern Chinese peoples from the barbarian hordes of Outer Mongolia. Winding through the mountains for a distance of 6,700 km. (4,200 mi.), it was constructed to follow carefully the topography of the country, to ensure the holding of strategic points in any battle. There are citadels, or watch towers, two stories high, about every 140 m., and a road runs along the top which was used for the movement of troops, as well as for more peaceful purposes at a time when communications in so wild an area were difficult. At Bada Ridge, to the northwest of Beijing, the wall has been meticulously restored to its original appearance; its average height at this point is 7 m. (23 ft.), and its width about 5.7 m. (18.8 ft.) at the top.

6. The capital today

The layout of the new city of Beijing follows the traditional Chinese symmetrical pattern, with Tienanmen, the great square that lies outside the Forbidden City, as its center. Here are the Monument to the Heroes of the People and, to the south, the Memorial to Chairman Mao, with the People's Assembly Hall on one side and the Museum of Revolutionary History on the other. Changan Street, Beijing's main thoroughfare, stretches east and west from Tienanmen like two huge arms uniting the city. To the east of Tienanmen are the newly built Beijing Hotel, as well as the embassy buildings, apartments for foreign diplomatic personnel, the International Club, and the international Friendship Store.

The old quarters of Beijing, where once the common people lived and worked, are today in an active process of reconstruction that reaches right out to the suburbs of the city. Spreading out from around the old imperial court and the structures and open spaces associated with it, new buildings are going up everywhere. The northwest suburb is the scientific and cultural center, with the Academy of Sciences and other such institutions spreading to the west, while the eastern and southern suburbs are the new industrial districts. An underground railway is in operation, and there is a spacious ring road around the city with trees on both sides, as well as many gardens dotted among the buildings of the city itself. At the same time large sums have been set aside for the repair and reconstruction of many historic sites and beauty spots. The large ancient buildings at present in restoration number almost a hundred. Many of them are receiving attention for the first time in several centuries. In the suburbs more than a dozen large reservoirs have been built, as well as innumerable smaller ones, so that the water from the Guang Ting and Mi Yün reservoirs can flow uninterruptedly into Beijing.

In its long history Beijing had always been a huge consumer city, but we have now developed a relatively complete industrial system that has gradually changed it from a consumer city to a productive one. Beijing's handicrafts, curios, scrolls, drawings, and objects of art command a worldwide market and are admired by people of all countries.

Beijing also has the largest library in the country, as well as the Imperial Palace Museum, an art gallery, and an exhibition pavilion. There are more than fifty colleges and universities; among them Beijing University and Qinghua University are well known throughout the world.

The new Beijing International Aerodrome, with up-to-date equipment, is now complete, and includes two runways 3,800 m. (12,500 ft.) in length designed for large jet planes. Inside the huge and spacious aerodrome building are murals of "The White Snake," "Nazha Invoking the Seas," and "The Water Sprinkling Festival," tokens of welcome to our friends from all parts of the world.

5/6. *The Great Wall, starting from Shanhaiguan, Hebei, in the east and ending at Jiayuguan, Gansu, in the west, stretches across six provinces and two autonomous regions to a total length of 6,700 km. (4,200 mi.). It is sometimes called "the long wall of 10,000 li." Here is a section crossing the Bada Ridge near Beijing, which has been repaired and restored to its original appearance of more than 2,000 years ago.*

7

7. Monument, with the Emperor Qian Long's inscription "Morning Moon at Lugou," standing by the Lugouqiau Bridge on the southwestern side of Beijing. The bridge was begun in 1189, during the Jin dynasty, and completed in 1192.

8. At the southern foot of Mount Jundushan, county of Changping, are scattered the tombs of the thirteen emperors of the Ming dynasty. This is the Ding Tomb, the first to be discovered (1956). It takes the form of an underground palace, and is now open to the public as the Ding Museum.

9. Zhoukoudian is on the southwestern outskirts of Beijing. This is where the fossils of Peking Man, half a million years old, were unearthed in 1929.

8

9

10. The Memorial to Chairman Mao in Tienanmen Square.

11. The cluster of buildings outside Jiangguomen seen from the ancient observatory.

12. The great square called Tienanmen in the center of Beijing. In the background is the entrance to the Forbidden City. The wide road in the foreground is Changan Street. Running from Jiangguomen in the east to Fuxingmen in the west, it is known as "the long street of 10 li" (5.76 km., or 3.6 mi.).

11

10

12

13

14

15

16

13/16. *The Long Corridor in the Summer Palace.*

14/15. *The Dragon Crown of the emperor, made of gold thread (14), and the Phoenix Crown of the empress (15), now exhibited in the museum in the Ding Tomb.*

17. *Detail of the Nine Dragon Screen in Beihai Park, Beijing. The screen is a mosaic of glazed bricks and tiles in seven colors, with nine curling dragons on either side. It was built in 1756.*

18

19

18. *Beihai Park at the northwestern side of the Imperial Palace. It was used for extra court accommodations in the Liao, Jin, and Yuan dynasties, and was turned into an imperial garden during the Ming and Qing dynasties. The white Tibetan Dagoba on the islet of Qionghuatao was built in 1651.*

19. *View of the top of the wall which surrounds the Imperial Palace. The palace, formerly known as the Forbidden City, has now become the Palace Museum. It is in the center of Beijing and occupies an area of 720,000 sq. m. (178 acres). The wall, over 10 m. (33 ft.) high with a moat more than 50 m. (165 ft.) wide, has uniquely designed watch towers at its four corners.*

20. *Bronze lion in the Imperial Palace.*

20

21. *General view of the Imperial Palace, showing the magnificent Taihe Dian (Hall of Supreme Harmony), where the emperor conducted the main business of state.*

22

22. *The new Beijing Roast Duck Restaurant has forty-one dining rooms and can cater to 5,000 customers a day. "Peking duck" is scorched outside so that the skin is crisp but the flesh inside still tender. It is cooked over wood from peach and other fruit trees, which gives the meat a peculiar fragrance.*

23. *Candied haws (hawthorn fruit) on sticks are popular with Beijing children, especially in winter.*

24. *The Temple of Heaven is the largest of its kind in China. The principal building is the Hall of Prayer for Good Harvest (Qilian Dian), 38 m. (125 ft.) high and 30 m. (99 ft.) in diameter. It is supported by twenty-eight pillars without any crossbeams, an early triumph of Chinese architectural skill.*

25. *The Imperial Vault of Heaven in the Temple of Heaven, showing the system of dougongs, or brackets, inserted between the top of the columns and the structural beams of the dome.*

23

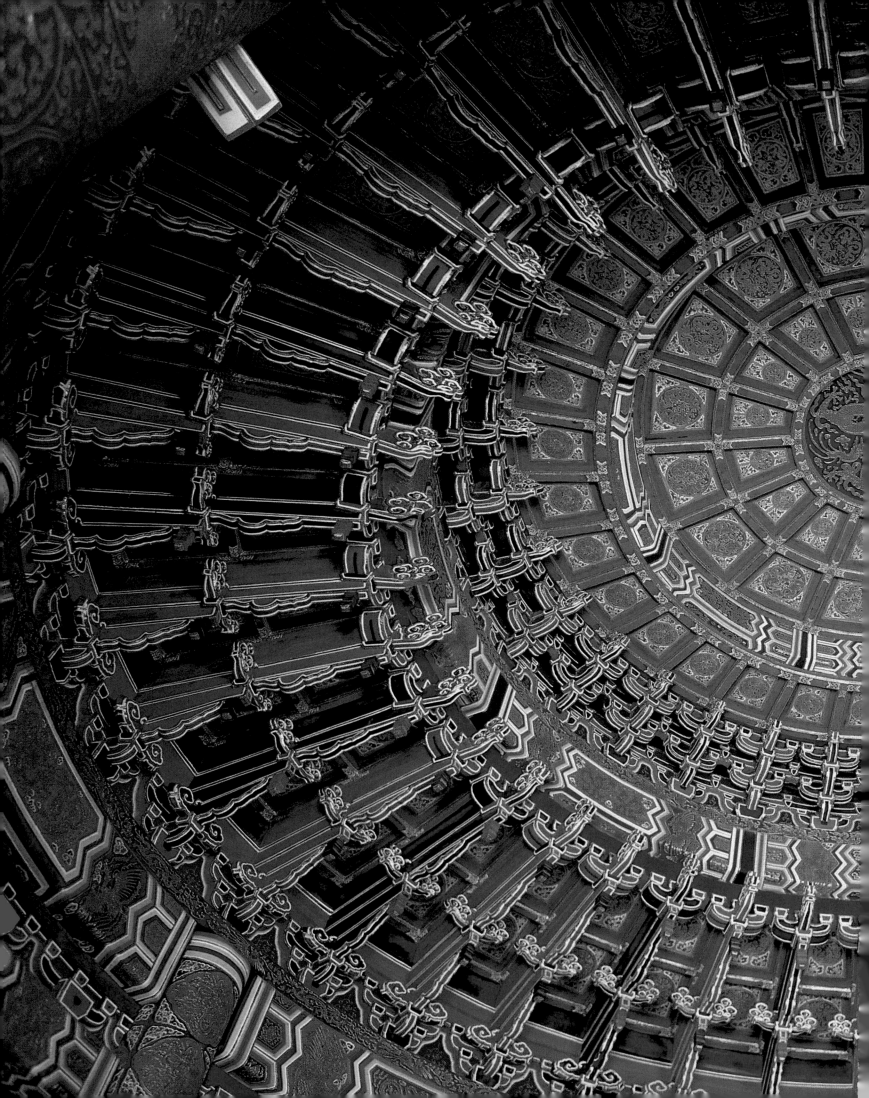

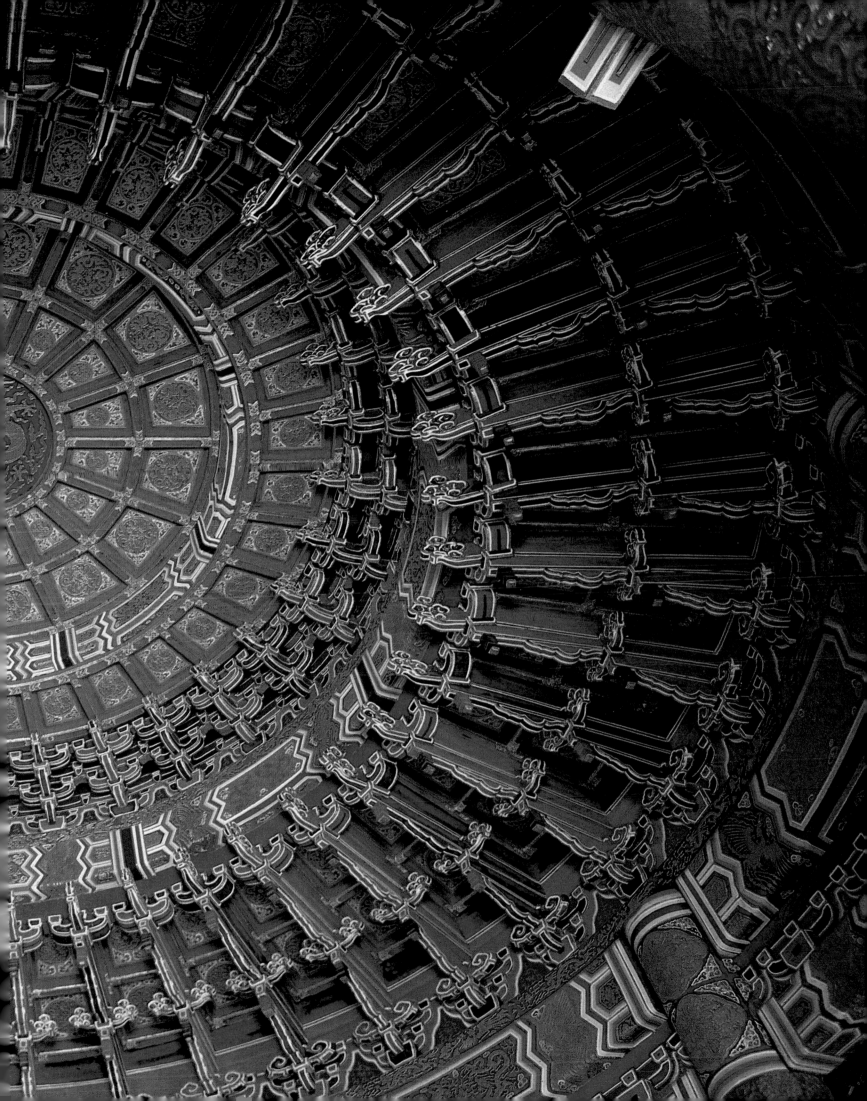

26

50

26. The Qianqing Gong (Palace of Heavenly Purity), the emperor's living quarters.

27. Jade dress unearthed from a tomb of the Western Han dynasty (206 B.C.—24 A.D.), on exhibition in the Palace Museum. The jade dress, worn by emperors or aristocrats after death, can be classified according to whether it is sewn with gold, silver, or copper thread. This one is made of 2,498 pieces of jade, sewn together with 1,100 grams (3.2 lb.) of gold thread.

28. Peking Opera has become famous all over the world for its charming costumes, delightful music, exquisite acting, and graceful dance movements. In content and execution it is strictly formalized, and concentrates on four main roles—the male, the female, the "painted face" (or deceiver), and the clown. The picture shows a female character type in appropriate costume and make-up.

29. During the Spring Festival—the Chinese New Year—the people round Beijing celebrate in the old traditional ways.

30. The Jingang Baozuo Pagoda (Pagoda of the Precious Seats of Buddha's Warriors), in the Blue Cloud Temple at the foot of Fragrance Hill (Xiangshan). The temple was extended on a large scale in 1748, during the Qing dynasty.

1. The Great Wall
2. The new harbor
3. The grasslands of Inner Mongolia
4. Treasures of Buddhist art
5. Other ancient buildings
6. The Imperial Summer Resort and the Eight Outer Temples

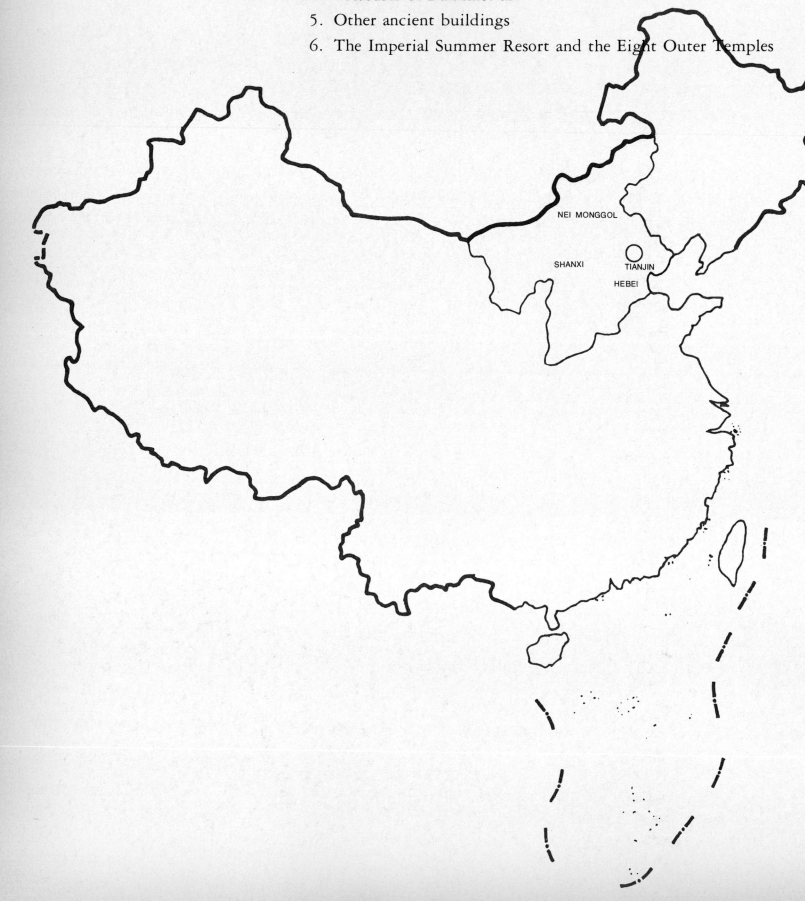

North China comprises Inner Mongolia (which is now the Autonomous Region of Nei Monggol), the provinces of Shanxi (Shansi) and Hebei (Hopeh), and the two cities of Beijing and Tianjin (Tientsin). It has an area of more than 1,760,000 sq. km. (680,000 sq. mi.) and a total population of 75 million (excluding Beijing and Tianjin, which come directly under the jurisdiction of the central government). This region was the cradle of ancient Chinese culture.

The topography of North China is such that the mountain ranges of Yanshan and Taihangshan make a dividing line between the highlands and the plains; to the south and east lie the plains of Hebei (also called the Haihe River plains), to the north and west are the Shanxi highlands, the mountainous district of north Hebei and the plateaus of Inner Mongolia. The mountains average from 1,000 to 2,000 m. (from 3,300 to 6,600 ft.) above sea level, with the northern peak of Wutaishan as the highest point (3,058 m., or 10,091 ft.). Wutaishan is famous as a sacred place for Chinese Buddhists, and Mount Heng (2,017 m., or 6,656 ft.) is one of the Five Sacred Mountains of China. The strategic importance of the Taihangshan Mountains made them a famous revolutionary base during the Sino-Japanese War.

Fertile and beautiful, North China is the largest wheat- and cotton-producing area in China, and the grasslands of Inner Mongolia form the biggest prairie. It is also a region of many different ethnic types, who have labored hard and created a culture that has made North China today a treasure house of historic sites and scenic beauties.

1. The Great Wall

On the coast of the Bohai Sea is the ancient town of Shanhaiguan. Being on the main line of communication between North China and the northeast, it has obvious strategic importance, and has been known from time immemorial as "the key to the capital." This is the eastern starting point of the Great Wall of China which, rising or falling like a huge dragon moving among the mountains, stretches westward for 6,700 km. (4,200 mi.) as far as Jiayuguan in the province of Gansu. Jiayuguan, the gateway into Xinjiang, is the western counterpart of Shanhaiguan.

The Great Wall is the most astonishing architectural achievement of ancient China. As far back as 400 B.C., during the time of the Warring States, the kingdoms of Chu, Wei, Yan, Zhao, and Qin had built walls at different strategic points for defense against each other. After the first of the Qin emperors had defeated his rivals and brought about the first unification of China, the northern walls of Qin, Zhao, and Yan were repaired and joined together in 214 B.C., as a bulwark against the invasion of the Xiongnu aristocracies. After the overthrow of the Qin emperors, succeeding dynasties—the Han, the Northern Wei, the Northern Qi, the Northern Zhou, and the Sui—added to the walls on their northern borders where they came into contact with the nomadic groups of Mongolia. During the Ming dynasty (1368–1644) the Great Wall, at this time

generally called "the boundary wall," was rebuilt no less than eighteen times as a defense against the Tartar and Wala peoples. The wall was divided into nine posts, or "borders," those now in North China being Ji Post, Xuanfu Post, Datong Post, and Shansi Post. The most important passes are at Shanhaiguan, Juyongguan, Pinxingguan, and Yanmenguan. Juyongguan is no more than 50 km. (31 mi.) from Beijing, in a deep valley with mountain ridges on both sides. The average height of the Great Wall is from 5 to 10 m. (from 16.5 to 33 ft.) and the width from 5 to 8 m. (from 16.5 to 26.4 ft.); at the top there are parapets on each side with a roadway in the middle, and about every 140 m. (462 ft.) there is a citadel for observation.

The immensity of the work and the hardship involved in this enormous undertaking are unthinkable. In ancient times there were no cranes, no facilities for transportation. Whence came the strength and the means with which these people were able to move megaliths weighing almost a ton each to such mountainous regions and erect them there in such numbers? There is only one answer: the amazing ingenuity and determination of those ancient builders, prepared to make any sacrifice and literally fling away human lives in this superhuman effort to protect their homeland. No wonder the Great Wall is said to be haunted by the ghosts of thousands upon thousands of workers who died during its construction. Yet it was done, and it has endured and still stands today as a symbol of the lasting strength of the Chinese people.

2. The new harbor

The Haihe River is 72 km. (45 mi.) long and forms the outlet for a group of waterways—the River Ziyahe, the River Daqinhe, the Southern Canal, the River Yongdinghe, and the Northern Canal—which all meet in the city of Tianjin. In the past, on account of the short distance from the source and the narrowness of the river bed downstream, the waters of the Haihe could not flow freely to the sea, so that in wintertime it usually overflowed and caused disastrous floods. After the Revolution, four large reservoirs were built to contain the excess water, and the channel of the Haihe was widened and deepened. As a result, there is no further flooding, and where the Haihe joins the sea is the new and flourishing harbor of Tanggu.

The city of Tianjin is a center of communications as well as one of the main industrial bases in China. In the past, the narrow, winding section of the Haihe which linked it with Dagukou was often frozen for two to three months in winter, so that navigation was greatly impeded. Dr. Sun Yatsen long ago advocated the construction of "a great northern port" in this area, but only now, after the Revolution, has this dream been realized. The oil pipes from Daqing now reach Qinhuangdao; the completion of the new harbor has made possible the anchorage of several ships of over 60,000 tons, and Tanggu has become the principal Chinese port for the export of coal and petroleum. On the coast of the Bohai Sea, where once a few poor fishermen struggled to gain a meager livelihood, the oilworkers of today have opened the gates to a treasure house of riches hidden beneath the bustling activity of China's newest port.

3. The grasslands of Inner Mongolia

Mongolia is famous throughout the world as the home of the great Khans of the thirteenth century. The founder of the Mongolian empire, Genghis Khan (1162–1227), was the first to give a real national structure to the people of this wild region: crossing the Great Wall into China, he sacked Beijing in 1215, and died leaving his grandson Hubilie (Kublai Khan) to found the Yuan dynasty with its capital in that city. But the Mongol empire only survived until 1368, and over the centuries since then the development of Mongolian nationality has been slow.

As it is now defined, the Autonomous Region of Nei Monggol, or Inner Mongolia, has a total of more than 1,400,000 sq. km. (550,000 sq. mi.), and from the Greater Xingan Ridge in the east to the Yinshan Mountains stretches a vast expanse of green as far as the eye can see. Everywhere is natural, rich prairie. "Vast is the sky, boundless the wilds; the grass is swept low by the wind. Everywhere are cattle and sheep." Here for countless centuries the famous Shanhe horses and Shanhe cattle have been the staple breeds of the Mongolian grasslands, and the fertile plains of Hohhot and the Great Bend of the Huanghe (Yellow River) a rich source of grain. In 1947 Inner Mongolia was set up as the first autonomous region in China, and its peoples' long-cherished hope for self-government was turned to reality. Since then, the peoples of Inner Mongolia have built up their own industry, in particular the important forest industry of the Greater Xingan Mountains, a region also rich in deposits of coal and iron and an excellent base for the development of a modern steel industry.

Hohhot, the name of the capital of the Inner Mongolian Autonomous Region, means in Mongolian "the green city." Close to it is the famous tomb of Wang Zhaojun of the Western Han dynasty. Known as one of "the four great beauties" of ancient times, Wang Zhaojun was selected to be sent to the Imperial Palace of Emperor Yuan Di of the Han dynasty. In the year 33 B.C. Huhanxie Chanju, of the neighboring Xiongnu people, demanded marriage with a Chinese girl as one of the terms of peace with the Han rulers, and Zhaojun volunteered for the position in the interests of political harmony. This story has been handed down as an example of the friendship that existed between the different nationalities in ancient times.

4. Treasures of Buddhist art

There are many charming and interesting mythical stories connected with Buddhism, and ever since its introduction into China in the year 67 A.D. its influence on Chinese art and culture has been profound. In particular, the many works of art produced by stone carving in ancient times are inseparably associated with Buddhism.

Among the most curious of these are the stone caves carved on the slopes of the mountains to form Buddhist shrines literally hewn from the solid rock. The carving of stone caves began as early as the fourth century and reached a peak in the Northern Wei, the Sui, and the Tang dynasties. Inside the caves were sculptured figures of the Buddha or, where the texture of the stone was not suitable for carving, images of the Buddha painted on the walls or made from clay.

The most famous stone caves in North China are at Yunggang in the Wuzhou Mountains, about 16 km. (10 mi.) from the industrial city of Datong; carved in the fifth century, they already have a history of some 1,500 years, and are the earliest and largest Buddhist caves in China. When the Northern Wei established their capital at Datong, they brought in Buddhism as the state religion, and one after another this series of grottoes was hewn from the cliffs, the principal ones between about 460 and 490 A.D., before the capital was moved on to Loyang. Today the caves number altogether fifty-three, stretching for about a kilometer, not quite two-thirds of a mile, east and west, and contain a total of 5,100 images of the Buddha ranging from 2 cm. to over 17 m. (56 ft.) in height. Many of the figures were carved in accordance with the myths and legends of the Buddhist religion, and afford precious research material for the study of ancient Chinese architecture, costumes, and music.

Another treasure house of Buddhist art is to be found at the monastery of Wutaishan, to the northeast of the county of Wutai in the province of Shanxi. Wutaishan is one of the Four Sacred Places of Buddhism, and it is said to be here that Wenshu Buddha preached his sermons. The architectural style of the monastery is varied in the extreme, with wooden structures of the Tang, Jin, and Yuan dynasties, and consequently provides invaluable material for the study of the history of Chinese architecture. The monastic buildings are of two kinds: those colored green, which house the monks wearing green robes, and those colored yellow, where the yellow-robed lamas have their homes. There are at present some forty temples attached to the monastery.

More important even than this, in ancient days, was the monastery of Fuguang—at least if we are to believe the tradition which says, "First comes the Fuguang Temple, then Wutaishan." Originally built in the reign of the Emperor Wen Di (471–499) of the Northern Wei dynasty, Fuguang was enlarged in the Tang period. The temple is constructed on the side of the mountain, and the figures of the Buddha are particularly vivid. Among other Buddhist monasteries in the region are the Nanchan monastery of the Tang dynasty, which contains the earliest wooden structure still remaining in China, the Yanqing monastery of the Jin dynasty, and the Guangji monastery of the Yuan period—all of them precious remnants of the ancient architecture of the Buddhist religion.

5. Other ancient buildings

Among the many fascinating architectural survivals in this rich area of China, one of the most remarkable is the Zhaozhou Bridge over the River

Jiaohe in the province of Hebei. Built in the reign of the Emperor Da Ye (605–616) of the Sui dynasty, it crosses the river in a single span of more than 37 m. (122 ft.) and is the oldest stone-arch bridge still in use in the world today. It was designed by the famous craftsman Li Chun of the Sui dynasty, and conforms to modern scientific principles in its structure and masonry. The arch is supported by twenty-eight huge parallel stones, with four small arches above it: these not only lighten the weight of the structure but also save material and facilitate the flow of water in case of flood. On the stone balustrades to either side of the bridge are carved dragons and animals in various postures as if they were in motion. The Zhaozhou Bridge was thoroughly overhauled in 1955 and now looks as magnificent as on the day it was built.

North China has more ancient buildings and historical relics than any other region of China. The Zhaozhou Bridge, the Wooden Pagoda of Yingzhou in the province of Shanxi, the Iron Lion of Cangzhou, and the Shengding Buddha at the monastery of Lungxin are together known as "the four treasures of North China." Then there is the Jin Temple of Taiyuan, in the province of Shanxi, built in the reign of Tien Bao (742–755), in the Sacred Lady's Hall of which is kept the exquisitely carved statue of a maid-in-waiting of the Song dynasty (960–1126). And there is the Palace of Yonglu, a Taoist building in the county of Rui, containing many wall paintings of the Yuan dynasty of great artistic value.

6. The Imperial Summer Resort and the Eight Outer Temples

Chengde is a well-known summer resort in the northern part of the province of Hebei, 250 km. (160 mi.) from Beijing. Its northern area consists of a series of large summer mountain villas, built in the reigns of the Emperors Kang Xi (1662–1722) and Qian Long (1736–1795) of the Qing dynasty. At the foot of the mountains are scattered a number of temples which combine the architectural styles of the various nationalities of China and are known as the Eight Outer Temples.

The Imperial Summer Resort itself is twice the size of the Summer Palace of Beijing, and is surrounded by a wall 10 km. (6.3 mi.) long. Begun in the early eighteenth century and renovated and enlarged over a period of eighty years, it may be divided into two main areas, the palaces and the gardens. The palaces are on the south side and are four in number: the Central Palace, the Pavilion of Pine and Crane, the palace known as the Wind from the Pines in All the Gullies, and the East Palace. These buildings, of plain bricks and tiles, are half hidden among clumps of tall, ancient trees. The Emperors Kang Xi and Qian Long, and later emperors of the Qing dynasty, spent five or six months every year here, managing the affairs of the state, receiving the chiefs of minority nationalities, and conferring with high officials and foreign diplomats. The Imperial Summer Resort became a second political center for China in the early Qing dynasty.

The gardens are divided into the lake district, plain district, and mountain district. The lake district depends largely on the River Rehe for its water,

using dikes, pavilions, and small bridges to divide it into different areas. Even in wintertime the spring water from the Rehe steams like a mist. The plain district is entirely covered with grass. Here, in the past, emperors of the Qing dynasty used to have picnics with Mongolian princes and watch the wrestling and shooting on horseback which were the favorite pastimes of the nomadic peoples. The mountain district has no less than seventy-two numbered views, with inscriptions by Kang Xi and Qian Long. Looking down from a high point, "Everywhere are clouds and mountains" and "The snow-covered South Lake" will come into view; looking to the south east, one will see "A thump with the club" and the Arhat (an Arhat is a Buddhist who has passed into Nirvana). The scenery of the lake changes constantly. Islands are dotted about like a natural painting on a screen.

The Eight Outer Temples are at the foot of the mountains on the east and north sides of the Summer Resort. The construction and decoration of these temples continued for almost seventy years, and they combine many of the characteristics of the culture and art of the Han, Tibetan, and Mongolian nationalities. For instance, the Pavilion of Mahayana in the Puning Temple has five tiers of eaves and five stories of square kiosks on the top. Inside the pavilion there is a wooden Avalokitesvara, a Buddha of mercy, with a thousand hands, weighing 110 tons. The gilded tile roof and the four golden dragons with upturned heads on the roof of the Temple of Happiness and Longevity are still bright and dazzling. In the Putuozhong-cheng Temple are preserved many historical relics and engraved tablets.

An immense amount of human labor and materials were lavished on the construction of the Summer Resort and the Eight Outer Temples. The gold used on the roof tiles of five of the temples alone amounted to 30,000 Chinese ounces. There was a popular saying, "The Summer Resort is truly a summer resort, but the people still sweat in the river."

All the same, it has to be said that there is no end to the beauties of the scenery here, and the Imperial Summer Resort is like Beihai, a "fairyland on earth."

31. *Xiaoling, the tomb of Shun Zhi, the first emperor of the Qing dynasty, at the foot of the Changrui Mountains. One of fifteen tombs of the Qing dynasty in the province of Hebei.*

32

33

32. Caisson ceiling of one of the Eight Outer
Temples, which stand at the foot of the
mountains to the north and east of the Imperial
Summer Resort.

33. The Iron Lion of Cangzhou in the province
of Hebei. The cast-iron lion is 6 m. (19.8 ft.)
both in length and height. A lotus seat on its
back bears the words "The Lion King."

34. Water Center Bower in the Imperial
Summer Resort. The Summer Resort, where the
emperors of the Qing dynasty spent the hot
months of the year, was built in the eighteenth
century. It has an area of 560 sq. m. (6,220
sq. ft.).

35

35. *Sculpture of Bodhisattva at Dulesi (the Temple of Solitary Joy) in the Ji district of Tianjin. Dulesi is one of the most famous ancient Chinese wooden buildings. It was first constructed in the Tang dynasty, and was rebuilt in 984 in the Liao dynasty. All that is now left is the gate and the Pavilion of Bodhisattva.*

36. *Clay sculpture of a maidservant of the Song dynasty, one of forty-two exquisite figures preserved in the Jin Temple. Each figure is arrayed in a vividly colored costume, and exhibits a different quality of temperament.*

37

38

37. *The Jin Temple was built by Tang Shuyu, the founder of the state of Jin. In the temple are the Hall of the Sacred Lady, the Memorial Temple of Tangshu, and the Temple of Guandi.*

38. *The Zhaozhou Bridge, also called Anziqiao (the Bridge of Safety and Relief), is the oldest stone-arch bridge still in use. It was designed by Li Chun in the early seventh century.*

39. *The Temple of the Twin Pagodas, originally called Yunzuosi, stands to the south of the village of Haozhuong on the outskirts of Taiyuan. It was built in the period of Wan Li (1573–1602) in the Ming dynasty. Both pagodas have thirteen stories and are 50 m. (165 ft.) high.*

40

40. *The Tayuansi (the Tower Temple) at Qingmiao in Wutaishan. The White Dagoba is 63.6 m. (210 ft.) high.*

41. *A Buddha in the Yunggang grottoes. There are now fifty-three grottoes at Yunggang, with 5,100-odd Buddhist idols and flying Apsaras. This Buddha is the earliest at Yunggang, in the twentieth grotto, and measures 13.75 m. (45.4 ft.) in height.*

42. *The Hanging Temple of Hunyuan. Constructed in the Northern Wei dynasty and rebuilt in the Qing dynasty, the buildings are supported on wooden pillars, with hanging cliffs above and a deep valley below.*

43. *Detail from the frescoes at Yunglegong (the Palace of Everlasting Happiness) in the province of Shanxi. These frescoes cover more than 800 sq. m. (8,800 sq. ft.). Dating from the Yuan dynasty, they develop the techniques of the Tang and Song dynasties before them.*

41

42

45

46

44. *The Wooden Pagoda of Yingzhou,
originally called the Sakya Pagoda, was built
in 1056. It is an octagonal building with six
tiers of eaves, about 67 m. (221 ft.) in height.*

45. *The Jingang Stupa, inside the Wutasi
(Temple of Five Pagodas) in Hohhot, was built
in the reign of Qian Long (1736–1795), and
is engraved with Buddhist texts in Sanskrit,
Tibetan, and Mongolian.*

46. *The tomb of Wang Zhaojun, a maid of
honor in the Imperial Palace of Emperor Yuan
Di of the Western Han dynasty, at Hohhot.*

47. *Lassoing horses on the steppes of Inner
Mongolia.*

48. *Hunting is still an important feature of life in these regions. The Handa moose, a rare species of the deer family, lives in the ice and snow of the Greater Xingan Mountains.*

49. *Extensive grasslands cover one-third of the area of the Inner Mongolian Autonomous Region, especially in the center and northeast. The luxuriant herbage makes rich fodder for cattle and sheep.*

50. *Wedding ceremony on the Erduosi prairie. Presents of woven silk are being exchanged with friends and relatives.*

49

50

1. The history of the region

2. A great industrial base

3. The three treasures, and others

Dongbei, which used to be known as Manchuria, is a large region in the northeastern part of China. It consists of three provinces—Liaoning, Jilin (Kirin), and Heilongjiang (Heilungkiang)—with a population of approximately 10 million. Its inhabitants are of various racial origins and include Han, Man (Manchu), Chaoxian (Korean), Monggal (Mongolian), Hui, Daur (Tahur), Oroqen (Olunchun), Hezhen (Hoche), Xibe (Sibo), and other peoples. The total area of the region is over 700,000 sq. km. (270,000 sq. mi.). It is a country of many mountains, rivers, and vast expanses of fertile land, rich in forest reserves and mineral resources, and with a well-developed industry. But before the establishment of the new China, this beautiful land was often devastated by foreign invaders. Then in 1948 the Communist Party liberated the whole region, and Dongbei returned to the hands of the Chinese people.

1. The history of the region

Dongbei is often called Bai Shan and Hei Shui (White Mountains and Black Waters), in reference to the snow-capped Changbai Mountains which stretch along the southeastern border of the province of Jilin and to the dark waters of the Heilongjiang River in the north. The name Heilongjiang actually means "black dragon." The river, seen from afar, appears like a coiling black dragon swimming through the hills.

The history of Dongbei can be traced back to very ancient times. As early as the old stone age human beings were already living there, and "Yu Shu Man," whose fossils were discovered in 1951, lived there in late paleolithic times tens of thousands of years ago. During the Period of the Warring States (475–221 B.C.), the areas of Liaoyang and Dushikou in the south were opened up to some extent, but no administrative body was yet established; at this time the mountainous district of Changbai and the river valley of the Heilongjiang were respectively the hunting grounds and pasturelands of nomadic Shushun tribesmen. At the time of the Tang dynasty, however, the Mohe tribe (the ancestors of the Manchus) established the state of Bohai, with its territory centering around Jilin and including the upper part of what is now called the Mudan River and the upper and middle reaches of the River Liao. The state of Bohai maintained friendly relations with the Tang rulers, and opened a new sea route between the peninsulas of Liaodong and Shandong. As a result, ideas and influences from the Central Plains flooded into the area, its economy developed, and it became representative of what is known as the Hai Dong (meaning "east of the sea") culture in Chinese history.

After the fall of the Tang dynasty, the state of Bohai also passed through troubled times and was conquered by the Qidan nomads, who established the Liao dynasty, only to be conquered in their turn by the Nuzhen peoples, who set up the powerful dynasty of the Jin (1115–1234). With the rise of Mongol power, both the Jin dynasty and the neighboring Song dynasty, which had been ruling central China for three centuries, fell before the northern invaders, and China was unified under the Mongolian emperors of the Yuan dynasty for the next hundred years.

Early in the seventeenth century, Nuerhachi, the chief of the Manchu peoples, became powerful and, taking advantage of the weakness of the last Ming emperor, invaded Beijing and in 1644 proclaimed the Qing dynasty, which continued to rule over the whole of China until the establishment of the republic in 1911. With the unification of China under the Qing rulers, many settlers from Shandong, Hebei, and Henan migrated to Dongbei, or Manchuria, as it was then called, and opened up the wastelands. As a result, the agriculture and economy of the region made great strides forward in the years of Manchu rule.

According to historical records, the peoples who established independent national groups during the confused history of Dongbei were the Han, the Man (Manchu), the Monggal (Mongolian), the Fuyu, and the Qidan. Of these the Han were the first, but it was the Man who chiefly dominated, particularly in later centuries. The Manchu capital of Shenyang still preserves the group of buildings erected by the Man people in imitation of the Forbidden City at Beijing, as well as two imperial mausoleums of the seventeenth century, but of the other nationalities who once lived and fought and established their capitals here very little trace remains.

The Imperial Palace in Shenyang, however, is China's largest imperial palace after the Forbidden City. Built between 1625 and 1636, in the reign of the Emperor Huantaiji, it covers an area of approximately 50,000 sq. m. (12 acres). At the entrance stand two tall and magnificent memorial archways, named Wen De Fang (the Arch of Merits in Civil Service) and Wu Gong Fang (the Arch of Military Accomplishments). The main group of buildings falls into east, middle and west sections. The chief building in the middle section is the Chong Zhen Palace (the Palace of Lofty Politics). This section was where the rulers of Qing dynasty held court, lived their daily lives, and offered sacrifices to their ancestors. In the east section, which has the Tai Zhen Palace (the Palace of Highest Politics) as its center, the emperors discussed important affairs of state, both political and military, with their ministers. The west section, with the Wen Yuan (Profound Knowledge Building) as its main part, was reserved for recreation and entertainment, study, and rest. All these buildings were magnificently decorated, with red walls and yellow tiles, upturned eaves and painted ridgepoles. The two mausoleums are the graves of Nuerhachi, the founder of the Qing dynasty (to the east), and of his son Huantaiji, the builder of the Imperial Palace (to the north). In front of the mausoleums, there is a pavilion with stone tablets. Behind the tablet pavilion is the Fang Chen (Square City), composed of various buildings including the Lung En Palace (the Palace of Great Favors).

In the last century, Dongbei has been invaded by the Japanese and the Russians, and in 1931 became a Japanese colony. Its recent history is the history of a devastated region and of a people fallen into the abyss of misery. But Dongbei was finally liberated in 1948, a year before the founding of the People's Republic of China. Since then, great changes have taken place. In the last thirty years industry, agriculture, animal husbandry, and fisheries have all gone ahead rapidly. The region has made great contributions to the rehabilitation and development of our country.

2. A great industrial base

Dongbei's natural conditions are extremely favorable for the development of modern heavy industries. It is richly endowed by nature and abounds in mineral and energy resources of various kinds. There are rich deposits of coal, petroleum, oil shale, iron, magnesium, molybdenum, copper, lead, zinc, aluminum, and gold. The iron mine in the area of Anshan and Bunqi is one of the biggest in China, with a deposit of more than 1 billion tons. The output of molybdenum from a mine in Jingxi is the largest in China, and the magnesium mine in Dashiqiao and gold mines scattered in the Heihe, Huma, and Tianbao Mountains are also important producers. Since the liberation, Dongbei has built up a comprehensive industrial system, with iron and steel, machine-building, petroleum, and petrochemical industries as its core. Other industries include coal, power, building materials, forestry, textile production, paper making, sugar refining, etc., and many industrial products from this region occupy a decisive position in the economy of our country. Dongbei accounts for one-third of China's production of iron and steel, as well as much mining and electricity-generating equipment and installations. Half of the country's petroleum, metallurgical equipment, automobiles, and timber are produced in this region.

The distribution of industry in Dongbei is becoming more and more rational, with iron and steel in Anshan and Bunqi; machine building in Shenyang, Luda, Changchun, Harbin, and Qiqihar; petroleum and petrochemical industries in Daqing, Jilin, and Fushun; coal in Fuxin, Fushun, Jinxi, and Hegau; timber in Jiamusi, Mudanjiang, and Yichun; and nonferrous metal smelting in Shenyang and Fushun.

Daqing is not to be found on a map, and is actually situated in the vast grasslands of the Song-Nen plains. This hitherto desolate wilderness has now become one of China's most important petroleum bases, and has verified the scientific analysis of the geological structure of eastern China made by Li Siguang (1889–1971), the famous Chinese geologist. With plain facts it refutes the erroneous assumption, held in the past, that China is an oil-poor country.

With industry developing so rapidly, a whole series of new cities, like Daqing and Anshan, have emerged in Dongbei. Some towns which were consumer-oriented in the past are now transformed into industrial centers turning out a wide range of products. For instance, the name Harbin means "sunning ground for drying fishnets" in the Manchu dialect, and sixty or seventy years ago Harbin was a small fishing village with only three fishing families living there. Now it is an industrial city, famous throughout China for its precision machine tools and electrical machinery, and winning praise at home and abroad for its linen mills, sugar-refining plants, and paper-making industries. Harbin is also known as "the city in green," because of the countless Chinese yellow scholar trees and cloves that have been planted along the sides of its broad boulevards. In summer, there is green all over the city and flowers give forth their fragrance everywhere, while in winter it is white with snow and turns into a silvery world. Or to

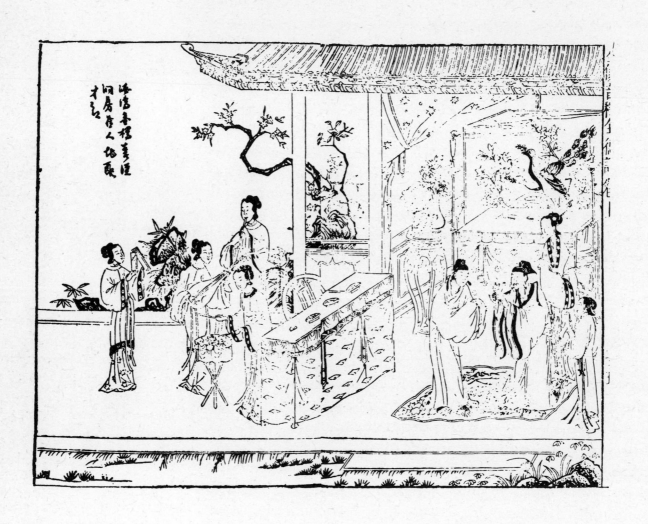

take another example, the name Qiqihar means "natural pasture" in the Daur (Tahur) dialect, but now its machine-building industry is second only to Harbin in the region.

Changchun is another new and developing city. At the end of the eighteenth century the site where it now stands was a sparsely inhabited wasteland, hunting ground and pasture country for Mongolian tribesmen. Before the liberation it was a typical consumer city. Today it has developed into an industrial city with engineering as its center, and has reached an advanced level in scientific and technological research. Jilin is picturesque and in the past has had practically no industry to speak of, but its basic chemical and power industries are rapidly developing. Shenyang (Mukden), the ancient capital of the Manchus, is a city of strategic importance, contested by many military strategists throughout the centuries. To its ancient renown it has now added the reputation for an engineering industry that is famous all over the country. On the coast at Luda is the big urban complex that includes the cities of Lushun (Port Arthur) and Dalien. Here the emphasis has been on shipbuilding, engineering, chemical-engineering, and textile industries. Bordering on the sea and surrounded on three sides by mountains, Dalien has enchanting natural scenery. It is well known as a sightseeing spot and health resort, with a port that is broad, deep, and ice-free. Huge seagoing vessels can berth at Dalien all the year round, and it forms, together with Lushun, Yinkou, and Huludao, one of "the four excellent harbors" of the country.

3. The three treasures, and others

Dongbei is the northernmost region of China. It is the nearest to the frigid zone and the furthest from the equator. Here the winter lasts very long, and the Heilongjiang River is frozen for six months of the year; in January, the temperature in most parts of Dongbei drops to −20°C. (−4°F.). The coldest spot of all is Mohe, on the banks of Heilongjiang, the "North Pole" of China, where the temperature once dropped to −52.3°C. (−62°F.). During March and April, when in the Changjiang (Yangtze) River valley the peaches begin to ripen and the willows put out new leaves, the wheat and barley in the fields turn green and the rape flowers blossom, snow and ice still cover the fields in Dongbei, and snowflakes are still swirling in the air. There is a poem widely known among the people of this northern world:

Only after spring is over do the flowers blossom;
The wheat comes to fulfillment as autumn ends.
Mountains amass the snow of a thousand years,
And even in June, frost is still on the ground.

It is a vivid description of the climate in Dongbei. In winter, frost and snow hang glittering on the branches of the trees in a thousand fantastic ways, and old pines towering majestically over the frozen fields are everywhere to be seen. It is difficult to imagine more magnificent northern scenery. Topographically, Dongbei is a basin surrounded by mountains and rivers; except for the southern part, which is open to the sea, it is hemmed in on all sides by high country. In the east are the forest-clad ranges of the Greater and Lesser Xingan. To the outer edge of the mountain areas, along the border, are valleys, with the Rivers Heilongjiang, Wusuli, and Yalu running through them like inlaid silver chains; within the mountain barriers are the vast, populous, and richly endowed plains of Dongbei. The Dongbei plains are centered in three main areas—the Sanjiang (Three Rivers), the Song-Nen (Songhua and Nen Rivers), and the Liaohe (the River Liao). They are all alluvial; the terrain is smooth and the soil fertile. The important agricultural products here include wheat, rice, maize, kaoliang (Chinese sorghum), and millet.

Among industrial crops, the output of soybeans, beets, flax, and sunflower seeds tops all other regions in the country. As to fruit, the main products are apples and pears from south and west Liaoning respectively; the total yield of apples in the province of Liaoning is higher than anywhere else in China. In the plains there is still a considerable expanse of uncultivated virgin land. In the past this was "the great northern wilderness," but today this vast area of virgin soil has been at least partially opened up by the pioneers from all parts of the country; state farms with a high level of mechanization have been established everywhere, and "the great northern wilderness" is becoming "the great northern granary," the grain reserve for the whole of modern China.

A large number of lakes (local inhabitants call them paozi—"small lakes"), as well as marshlands and swamps, are scattered over the Song-Nen and Sanjiang plains. After the end of April every year, golden pot marigolds and white Chinese herbaceous peonies are in full bloom among the thick growth of light green grass. This is excellent natural pastureland.

Dongbei has the richest forest reserve in China, with forested zones occupying 20% of its total area; its timber resources and lumber output are the biggest in the country. In these primeval forests, thousands upon thousands of trees reach to the sky; no wonder people call this area "the sea of woods." There are more than 300 species of trees growing in the Greater and Lesser Xingan Mountains and on the Changbai range, including at least eighty of the commoner varieties. Among the conifers there are larches, Korean pines, dragon spruces, and firs, and among broadleaf trees, oaks, birches, and elms—mostly with tall, straight trunks suitable for many uses. There are also a lot of rare trees, like the northeastern China ash, whose hard, smooth wood makes excellent material for precision tools and furniture.

The mountain areas and wooded zones provide not only an inexhaustible resource of timber but also many rare and precious wild animals and plants. Among these, the most important are the pine marten, ginseng, and pilose antler—known far and wide as "the three treasures of Dongbei." Pine martens (or sables), together with many other animals such as sikas (Chinese deer), tigers, otters, and bears, make their homes in the virgin forests. Due to the cold weather, their fur is soft, thick, and lustrous, and

ranks first in China both in quality and quantity. Pilose antler, the furry antler of the young deer, and ginseng, the famous Chinese rejuvenator, are highly prized for their medical virtues. Indeed, more than 300 species of wild medicinal herbs and plants are to be found in this region, as well as more exotic medicaments like tiger bone, bear's gallbladder, and musk. Among forest by-products, mushrooms, edible fungus, citrons, pine nuts, and mountain grapes are produced in large quantities; "monkey-head" mushrooms not only are delicious and nourishing, but are used in the manufacture of a kind of tumor-inhibiting medicine.

To the south of Dongbei lie the Huanghai (Yellow) Sea and the Bohai Sea, with a coastline 1,400 km. (875 mi.) long. The many rivers which pour large quantities of fresh water into these two seas make the content of salt rather low and the quantity of oxygen dissolved fairly high, and various sorts of nutritious salts are abundant. Further, the depth of both seas and the frequent sunshine make them especially suitable as spawning grounds for fish. Among the fresh-water fishes in this region, carp, including silver and black carp, are plentiful; there are also sturgeon, and at least ten species of salmon. The best among these is chum salmon; its flesh is reddish in color, short-fibered, and rich in fat and vitamins. A special delicacy is the san hua ("three flowers") fish of the Songhua River. Among sea fishes there are croakers, mackerel, hairtail fish, flatfish, prawns, and abalones; Bohai Bay teams with shrimps and crabs, and along the coast of the Huanghai Sea there are masses of sea slugs, sea cucumbers, and oysters. In the coastal waters, near Lushun, is an aquatic breeding district, where large quantities of sea slugs, sea cucumbers, tangles, and scallops are produced.

The Five Large Lotus Lakes and the Heavenly Lake high up on Mount Baitou are two of the most famous beauty spots in Dongbei. They add a touch of southern scenery to these magnificent northern landscapes. The Five Large Lotus Lakes are a string of lakes formed by congested river waters. The biggest of them is the third, with an area even larger than the West Lake in Hangzhou. The blue ripples of the water and the fourteen cone-shaped volcanoes scattered around the lake set each other off beautifully and create a magnificent effect. The Heavenly Lake is situated at the summit of Mount Baitou (the White Headed Mountain), which is the highest peak in the Changbai range. The lake, with a total area of 9.2 sq. km. (3.6 sq. mi.), is over 2,100 m. (6,900 ft.) above sea level. Its waters are clear and blue and, with the peaks of the surrounding mountains mirrored in its gently moving surface, make a sight that is unforgettable in its fantastic beauty.

Deep and limpid are the waters of the Heavenly Lake,
Rising one above the other the mountain peaks;
In the skies the wavering clouds flow gracefully by
And over the lake come 10,000 rainbows.

To the southern side of the lake is a gap known as Ta Meng (the Wicket Gate), through which the lake waters tumble down a gorge more than 1,200 m. (3,900 ft.) long and form a waterfall 68 m. (224 ft.) high, one of the biggest waterfalls in China.

51. *The Imperial Palace in Shenyang, province of Liaoning, built between 1625 and 1636. Its design shows characteristics of both Han and Man (Manchu) architectural styles. It occupies an area of approximately 50,000 sq. m. (12 acres), and is China's largest imperial palace after the Forbidden City in Beijing. The picture shows the interior of Qing Ning Palace (the Palace of Peace and Quiet).*

52

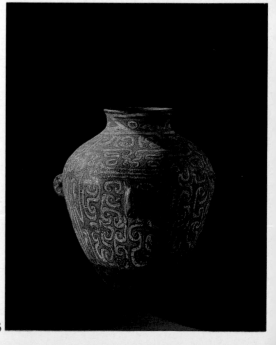

53

54

52. Chong Zhen Palace (the Palace of Lofty Politics) in the Imperial Palace at Shenyang, built for the Emperor Huantaiji (1627–1636) of the Qing dynasty to hold grand ceremonies.

53. This urn-shaped wine vessel with four hoops was discovered in a tomb of the early bronze age, in the Dadianzi Commune of the Han Banner, Zhaowuda League.

54. Zhao Ling (the Zhao Tomb, also called the North Tomb) is the grave of Emperor Huantaiji of the Qing dynasty. Its construction was started in 1643 and completed in 1651. It is the largest and best-preserved mausoleum of any of the first three emperors of the Qing Dynasty, the other two mausoleums being those of Fu Ling in Shenyang and Yong Ling in Xinbing. After the Revolution

the mausoleum became the North Tomb Park. The picture shows Lung En Palace (the Palace of Great Favors).

55. Part of Tai Zhen Palace (the Palace of Highest Politics) in the Imperial Palace at Shenyang.

56. The Qian Shan Mountains, also called Qian Hua (a Thousand Flowers) or Qian Duo Lian Hua (a Thousand Lotus Flowers). Spreading to the southeast of Anshan, they cover an area of approximately 300 sq. km. (120 sq. mi.). Many temples were built here from the Sui dynasty to the Qing.

57

58

57. *Fishermen harvesting kelp (a large brown seaweed) in the straits of the Bohai Sea. More than 100 km. (62 mi.) wide and up to 40 m. (132 ft.) deep, with a temperate climate, these are excellent waters for breeding fish and cultivating aquatic plants.*

58. *The coast at Luda. Its warm climate and other attractions make it a favorite summer resort for thousands of people every year.*

59. *Port Dalien. Broad, deep, and free from ice, this is one of China's busiest commercial ports and an important fishing base.*

60

60. The Heavenly Lake, 2,185 m. (7,211 ft.) above sea level in the Changbai Mountains. Covering a total area of 9.38 sq. km. (3.66 sq. ft.), and up to 373 m. (1,231 ft.) in depth, it is surrounded on all sides by mountain peaks.

61. Ginseng, the famous Chinese rejuvenator, is made from a root found in the remoter parts of the Changbai Mountains. It is also cultivated artificially, but the cultivated ginseng is considered inferior to mountain ginseng.

62. Sikas. The Chinese call them mehihua ("plumblossom") deer, after the blossom-like patterns on their hide. Male sikas grow antlers from their second year. Pilose antler and deer's placenta are considered rare and valuable medicines.

63. Living in the central part of the Hulunbeier region in the province of Heilongjiang, the Ewanki (Owank) people make their living by hunting. Before the Revolution this nationality was on the verge of extinction, with only 136 members left. Now it has grown to about 10,000.

61

62

63

64

65

64. A child calligrapher. Zhou Muying, aged six, is writing a horizontal scroll of calligraphy with a big brush.

65. Sable, a small rare animal, in the Dongbei region. It can survive in the ice and snow at temperatures as low as −50°C. (−58°F.) and its fur, soft and thick, has great economic value.

66. "Tree hangings" by the Songhua River. In the depth of winter, if the cold wind blows all through the night, then next morning silvery flowers of ice and snow blossom all over the city. Tree hangings herald happiness. There are sayings that "if tree hangings appear, we shall have fine weather for three days" and "if tree hangings come early, a bumper harvest will follow."

67. Mohe, the "North Pole" of China. Its latitude is 53°30′ North. It has long hours of daylight, and many tourists come from afar to see "the city without nights."

Chapter IV   East China—Huadong

1. Mountains and rivers

2. Historical sites

3. Pearls along the southeastern coast

Huadong is situated in the eastern part of the Chinese mainland and includes the city of Shanghai and seven provinces; Shandong (Shantung), Jiangsu (Kiangsu), Anhui (Anhwei), Zhejiang (Chekiang), Jiangxi (Kiangsi), Fujian (Fukien), and Taiwan. It is long from north to south but comparatively narrow from east to west, with a total area of over 800,000 sq. km. (310,000 sq. mi.). The population is around 230 million. Except for Anhui and Jiangxi, all the provinces, and Shanghai, border the sea. Many of the famous Chinese rivers, such as the Changjiang (the Yangtze), the Huanghe (the Yellow River), and the Huaihe, flow through this region on their way to the sea, and there are many fine bays and gulfs scattered along its extensive coastline. In the north, the Shandong Peninsula stretches out like an arm, enclosing the Huanghai (Yellow) Sea; to the south, the island of Taiwan stands like a sentry facing the Pacific Ocean. Here the climate is temperate, the population dense, and the products abundant. It is a region with a flourishing industry, well-developed agriculture, and advanced levels of culture and education.

1. Mountains and rivers

Unlike the western part of China, this region has no grand or majestic mountain ranges; rather, its provinces all abound in rivers and lakes. But even here, in the upland areas, unusual peaks and hills rise abruptly out of the ground, tall, graceful, and enchanting.

The northernmost province of the region is Shandong, an extension of the plains of Huabei that climbs, in its central districts, to the hilly terrain of the Shandong highlands. Here, rising to a height of 1,524 m. (5,029 ft.) above sea level, is the most famous of China's historic mountains, Mount Tai. Mount Tai is the first, and the easternmost, of the Five Sacred Mountains of China, taking precedence over Mount Heng (Hunan) in the south, Mount Hua in the west, Mount Heng (Hebei) in the north, and Mount Song in the center. To the Chinese it has been sacred and an object of reverence from time immemorial, and to it came kings and emperors as far back as Qin Shin Huang, the founder of the Qin dynasty, and Han Wu Di, who reigned in the second century B.C., to worship and pray to heaven and give thanks for peace and prosperity. Confucius climbed to the top and looked down: "From the summit of Mount Tai," he said, "you can truly feel the smallness of the world." To the people it is a symbol of strength and grandeur. "As solid as Mount Tai," they say. In a different vein, they say something like, "Even with his eyes open, he can't see Mount Tai."

In the central part of Huadong, south of the Changjiang, stretches a terrain of low, undulating mountains and hills, the northern edge of China's eastern highlands. Rising abruptly out of these is Mount Huang, in southern Anhui, a famous beauty spot. Originally called Mount Yi, it received its present name in the sixth year of the reign of the Emperor Tian Bao of the Tang dynasty (747 A.D.). Mount Huang has many peaks, of which no less than seventy-two have names. Both Lienhua (the Lotus Flower), which is the highest, and Tiandu (the Heavenly Capital) are over

1,800 m. (5,900 ft.) above sea level. Mount Huang is fascinating for its towering and grotesquely shaped rock formations, its hardy old pines, its clear and inexhaustible springs, and the rolling sea of clouds above it. Xu Xiake (1586–1641) eulogized Mount Huang in these words: "No other mountain will I look at after visiting the Five Sacred Mountains; no Five Sacred Mountains will I look at after visiting Mount Huang."

Another famous mountain, Mount Lushan, is situated in the northwestern part of the province of Jiangxi, where the Changjiang joins Lake Poyang. Standing tall and upright between lake and river, it has a circumference of 250 km. (156 mi.) and many high ridges. Mount Lushan owes its name to an ancient legend. It is said that thousands of years ago there was a certain Kuang family of seven brothers. They built cottages on the mountain and led the life of hermits there; later, all of them achieved a state of holiness, left the mountain, and became celestial beings, leaving their cottages behind. The people ever afterward called the mountain Lushan (the Mountain of Cottages) or Kuang (after the Kuang brothers), or even Kuang Lu (the Cottage of the Kuangs). Since the Jin dynasty many poets and men of letters have been infatuated with its beautiful scenery, and many poems have been written about it.

The Changjiang (Yangtze) delta, in the center of Huadong, is often mentioned as "the land of plenty." From ancient times it has been known as a land of rivers and lakes: except for a few isolated hills, the whole area is broad and smooth, with a height of not more than 10 m. (33 ft.) above sea level. Lake Taihu is the fourth largest fresh-water lake in China. It lies between the provinces of Jiangsu and Zhejiang, and is surrounded by more than 250 other lakes, large and small, scattered around it like sparkling pearls on the green fields. Lake Taihu and the lakeside city of Wuxi are a popular tourist center.

Rivers and streams spread all over Huadong, which has within its domain not only big rivers, such as the Changjiang, the longest river in China, and the Huanghe, but also many complicated smaller branches and streams. And apart from these, Huadong also has within its domain the Grand Canal, which in its way is as famous as the Great Wall. The canal, 1,794 km. (1,121 mi.) long, extended from Beijing in the north to Hangzhou, running through the provinces of Shandong, Jiangsu, and Zhejiang. It was built on the orders of the Emperor Yan Di (569–618) of the Sui dynasty, purely for his own pleasure trips down to Yangzhou to enjoy the sight of the qiong flowers (a very rare flower now extinct) which blossomed there. Nevertheless, by building the canal, this happy-go-lucky emperor quite unintentionally did a good deed to his people. The Grand Canal became a major artery of communications between north and south and promoted economic and cultural exchanges that helped to bring progress and prosperity to the regions along its banks.

2. Historical sites

Relics of the neolithic age have been discovered in all the provinces of Huadong, showing that human activities have been going on here for at least 5,000 years. The northern part of the region borders on the ancient culture of the Central Plains, and was therefore developed early. More than 2,000 years ago, during the Spring and Autumn Period and the Period of Warring States, Shandong was the domain of the dukedoms (later kingdoms) of Qi and Lu. Situated in north Shandong, bordering on the sea, Qi was a powerful state holding a vast territory of fertile land and economically very strong. With its capital at Yingqiu (now Linyi), it was the first eastern kingdom to seek authority over the Central Plains. To the south of it lay the kingdom of Lu, with its capital at Qufu. Here we can still find more than 300 cultural and historical relics, among them the remains of the ancient city built in Lu times, the Yan Temple (in honor of Confucius's disciple Yan Huei), the Temple of the Duke Zhou (in memory of the first Duke of Lu), and the Shaohao mausoleum. Qufu was also the birthplace of Confucius, and there are still many ancient buildings and gardens connected with him—the Confucian Temple, the House of the Confucian Family, the Confucian Gardens, etc. The Confucian Temple is a group of majestic buildings second only to the Forbidden City in size and splendor; their beautifully painted pillars and carved beams and the upturned eaves of their pavilions and rooftops reflect the great artistic achievements of ancient Chinese architecture. In the Confucian Gardens, among some 20,000 old pines and green cypresses, more than sixty pavilions, buildings, archways, and palaces can be dimly seen through the dense thickness of the trees. This is the largest and most ancient artificial garden still extant in East China.

In the fifth century B.C., during the later stages of the Spring and Autumn Period, two kingdoms sprang up around the lower reaches of the River Changjiang and in the Qiantang River valley. They were the kingdoms of Wu and Yue with their capitals at Suzhou (Soochow) in the province of Jiangsu and at Shaoxing in the province of Zhejiang respectively. Bordering on the sea and with acre upon acre of fertile land to call upon, their social and economic power developed quickly with the influx of ideas from the Central Plains, and they soon became the dominant powers in the southeastern China of the time.

Around 500 B.C., by order of He Lu, king of Wu (514–496 B.C.), a senior court official, Wu Zixu, undertook the construction of the city of Suzhou. It is said to have had a circumference of 40 li, or 20 km. (12.5 mi.). In the 2,400 years since then it has seen many changes and suffered many ups and downs, yet much has been preserved. Marco Polo visited Suzhou around 1280 A.D. and described it in his travel notes as "a big and beautiful city." He must have felt at home there, for Suzhou, like Venice, is built on water, with canals and waterways that still criss-cross the ancient town. Many houses have doors that open onto both streets and canals, and the characteristic hump-backed bridges are everywhere to be seen. Suzhou is often called "the Venice of the East." The country around it is also beautiful, with Mount Tianping (the Sky Flat Mountain), Mount Lingyan (the Fairy Rock), the Eastern and Western Dongting Mountains, etc. Nearer to Suzhou itself is the lake called Jian Chi (the Pond of Swords) on Hu Qiu Hill (Tiger Hill). It is said that this is the burial site of He Lu, who

loved double-edged swords when he was alive and had 3,000 double-edged swords thrown into his grave as funeral objects after his death, splitting the pond open as if by a single sword stroke and leaving its stone walls smooth, straight, and erect. Legend has it that after the burial a white tiger was seen on the hill, which gave rise to the name by which it has been known ever since.

Suzhou also boasts of many beautiful gardens, large and small. Among them Canglang (the Pavilion of Gentle Waves), Shizi Lin (the Lion Grove Garden), Zhuozhen Yuan (the Humble Administrator's Garden) and Liu (the Lingering Garden) form the Four Grand Gardens of Suzhou. They are laid out in the horticultural styles of the Song, Yuan, Ming, and Qing dynasties respectively, and though they are not so magnificently gorgeous as the palace gardens, they are still elegant and refined. Making use of the peculiarities of the surrounding landscape, they are ingeniously and often tortuously designed. For example, Shizi Lin was planned and constructed in the Yuan dynasty by ten well-known painters, including Ni Yunlin (1301–1374). Recently, Chinese experts made a replica of the Dianchunyi (the Hall for Staying Spring) in the Wang Shi Yuan (the Master of Nets Garden), a typical Chinese garden building of the Ming dynasty, for display in the Metropolitan Museum of Art in New York, to allow the American public to see and appreciate traditional Chinese gardening art. Generally speaking, though the Huadong region was developed to a certain extent during the Spring and Autumn Period, compared with North China it still lagged far behind. Up to the Qin and Han dynasties, the areas south of the River Huaihe were sparsely populated and their production level was comparatively low.

Toward the end of the Eastern Han dynasty (25–220 A.D.), peasant uprisings weakened the rule of the Han central administration, and three new kingdoms—Wei, Shu, and a second kingdom of Wu—emerged, dividing China into three parts. The lower reaches of the Changjiang and the province of Fujian were under the sovereignty of the kingdom of Wu where, owing to the excellent natural conditions and fertile soil of the area, the economy prospered. Because the people of Wu had to wage war on the waters of the Changjiang and equip themselves also for sea transportation, the kingdom became noted for its shipbuilding, and in fact sent commercial fleets to foreign countries, such as Korea and Indonesia. At first the capital of Wu was at Wu Chang, but later it was moved to Jiangye, now Nanjing (Nanking), the present-day capital of Jiangsu.

For many years after the disappearance of Wu, later dynasties continued to make Nanjing their capital: the Eastern Jin (317–420), and Southern Song (420–479), Qi (479–502), Liang (502–557), and Chen (557–589), and, after a long gap, the Later Tang (923–936) of the Period of the Five Dynasties. So Nanjing has a good claim to be regarded as one of China's most ancient capitals. The city is rectangular in shape, 10 km. (6.3 mi.) from south to north and 5.5 km. (3.4 mi.) from east to west, with a circumference of 33 km. (20.6 mi.). Situated at the meeting point of the Hubei-Hunan-Anhui and the Jiangsu-Zhejiang areas, Nanjing is in an extremely important strategic position. Our forefathers spoke of it as "a dragon coiling around Mount Zhong Shan, a tiger crouching in Shitou," and when it was liberated in 1949 Chairman Mao Zedong wrote these famous lines in celebration:

A tiger crouching, a dragon curling, the city now outshines its ancient glories,

In triump heaven and earth have been overturned.

At the foot of the Purple and Gold Mountain to the west of Nanjing stands the mausoleum of Dr. Sun Yat-sen, the great Chinese revolutionary leader, and outside the city there is a cemetery for the martyrs of the Revolution at Yu Hua Tai (the Rainflower Platform). Other places of special interest inside and outside the city include Lake Xuanwu, Yanzi Ji Rock, the Xiao Tombs of the Ming dynasty (1368–1644), and the Linggu Temple. The magnificent new Changjiang River Bridge, built after the liberation, spans the broad flood of the Changjiang at a point where it is fully 1,000 m. (3,300 ft.) wide. Double-decked, it links the Tianjin-Pukou and Nanjing-Shanghai railways as well as the highway networks on the north and south side of this great barrier of water.

People often use the phrase "the beauties of the six dynasties" when referring to the prosperity of Nanjing in the past. And it is true that this prosperity really began after the Eastern Jin dynasty made its capital there, and people started migrating southward in great numbers. This was the first large-scale migration of population in Chinese history, and it was this which really turned the plains of the lower and middle Changjiang into a rich and populous region. Even the valley of the Mingjiang (now the province of Fujian) was gradually weaned from its backward state. The building of the Grand Canal in the Sui dynasty, for all its frivolous imperial origin, also contributed greatly to the development of the south and, in particular, to the emergence of the city of Yangzhou.

Yangzhou is situated in the plains of north Jiangsu. Being near the mouth of the Changjiang, it became the collecting and distributing center for salt in the area of the River Huaihe, and its commercial activities were highly prosperous: its production of jade objects, lacquerware, and flowers made of wool, silk, and paper was known all over the country. The ancient lines "With a hundred strings of money in cash, we ride on cranes to Yangzhou" give a hint of its prosperity at this period, and other lines—"One moonlit night on the twenty-four bridges I heard a beauty teaching students to play the flute, but I never saw where"—conjure up a nocturnal picture of old Yangzhou, with lights glimmering here and there in the darkness. Today there are still many historical and cultural remains left from the days of the dynasties. To the northwest of the city lies Lake Shou Xihu (the Thin West Lake), long and narrow, with many nooks and recesses and beautiful flowers and trees on its banks. Jian Zhen (688–763), the famous monk of the Tank dynasty who in old age braved the seas to found a Buddhist sect in Japan, was head monk of the Da Ming Temple (now the Fa Jin Temple) in Yangzhou. A hall in his memory has been set up there, modeled on the Tang Zhao Ti Temple built by Jian Zhen himself in Japan.

If the Grand Canal brought prosperity to Yangzhou, even greater prosperity came to Hangzhou (Hangchow), at its southern end. This good fortune reached a climax under the Southern Song dynasty, which ruled over southeastern China from 1127 to 1279. Threatened by attacks from the Nuzhen people in the north, the Song emperors moved their political center southward to Hangzhou, on the north bank of the River Qiantang. It had already been the capital of the states of Wu and Yue during the Period of the Five Dynasties (907–960), and continued to be an important seaport during the Northern Song dynasty (960–1127). But above all it was a place where pleasure-seeking aristocrats and people from the upper classes sang and enjoyed themselves. The West Lake of Hangzhou has been praised by the poets of all ages, who knew it as "the pearl of the east." Surrounded on three sides by mountains, it is divided into the Inner and Outer Lakes, with a pavilion called Hu Xin Ting (the Mid-Lake Pavilion) at its center. On the mountains south of the lake there are many temples, pagodas, and stone carvings that reflect the varied artistic creativity of the Chinese people hundreds and even thousands of years ago. Among them, Liu-ying Temple is probably the most frequented by visitors from home and abroad. "There is a paradise in heaven," it is said, "but there are Suzhou and Hangzhou on earth."

In the period before the Yuan dynasty (1276–1368), there was a second large-scale migration from the north, which so increased the population of the lower and middle reaches of the Changjiang that many people moved out to the southern and eastern parts of the province of Jiangxi, and these desolate mountain areas were developed too. Nanchang, the provincial capital of Jiangxi, has been the site of the provincial administration ever since the Han dynasty, 206 B.C.–220 A.D.). On August 1, 1927, Zhou Enlai, Zhu De, He Lung, and other Chinese revolutionary leaders led an army revolt here, popularly known as the Nanchang uprising.

Its headquarters in the city have been preserved and a monument in commemoration recently erected in August 1 Square.

In the western part of Jiangxi in the Jinjiang Mountains, part of the Lo Xiao range, towers majestically Mount Jin Gang. On October 27, 1927, Mao Zedong and his comrades in arms led a revolutionary peasant army from Hunan to Mount Jin Gang and set up China's first rural revolutionary base there. This was the beginning of the seizure of state power by the armed forces, and the sparks of the revolutionary fire kindled on Mount Jin Gang developed, over the next twenty years, into the flames that covered the whole country. Relics of those times are everywhere to be seen on Mount Jin Gang, and a museum of revolutionary history was set up there after the liberation.

Since the victory of the people's revolution, the coastal area of Huadong has changed a great deal. After the Opium War of 1840, when Western imperialists used gunboats and cannons to compel China to open its doors, Fuzhou (Foochow), Xiamen, Ningbo, and Shanghai became bases for foreign infiltration of China. A semicolonial, lopsided economy thus developed all along the Huadong coastline. Since the establishment of the new China, however, this has all completely changed, and today the region of Huadong plays an important role in the social structure of the whole country.

3. Pearls along the southeastern coast

The long coastline of Huadong is studded with excellent harbors, and offshore islands are scattered over the sea like stars in the sky. Among them, the coastal city of Shanghai and the island of Taiwan are especially noteworthy.

Shanghai is situated at the mouth of the River Changjiang, just about at the middle point of the coast of China. With an area of 5,800 sq. km. (2,260 sq. mi.) and a population of about 11 million, Shanghai is the largest city in the country, and is divided into ten districts and ten suburban counties. In ancient times, it was a lonely fishing village, known in the Western Jin dynasty as Hu Du. Hu in Chinese is the name of a kind of bamboo railing used for catching fish, and Du means "ditch." Shanghai is still sometimes called Hu for short. The town of Shanghai was set up during the Song dynasty (960–1279), and became a flourishing seaport by the seventeenth century. After the Opium War foreign powers made Shanghai an important base for infiltration into China; every imperialist country established settlements and concessions here, stationing troops, setting up banks, police stations, and factories, occupying wharfs and controlling the Shanghai customs. Building after building rose up, factory after factory; boulevards and roads appeared. To the Chinese people all this only meant cruelty and oppression: Shanghai was indeed "a paradise for adventurers," the largest and most exploited metropolis in the Far East. But in May 1949 the city was at last liberated and returned to the hands of the people. Today Shanghai has become one of China's most important industrial bases. There are more than 10,000 factories and workshops with 2 million industrial workers, using advanced technology. Shanghai's light and textile industrial products are welcomed on the international market, and its exquisite and ingenious articles of art and handicrafts are famous at home and abroad.

Shanghai is also a city with a great revolutionary tradition. The First National Congress of the Chinese Communist Party, with twelve delegates (among them Mao Zedong), was held in Shanghai in 1921. While it was holding session, the Congress was detected by the enemy and had to move its meeting place to a boat on Lake Nanhu in the province of Zhejiang. Many precious places of the Revolution have been preserved here, among them the site of the First Congress and the house where Zhou Enlai set up his headquarters during the Shanghai workers' third uprising.

Dianchun Tang (the Hall for Summoning the Spring) in Yu Yuan (the Garden of Leisurely Happiness) was the headquarters of the Dagger Society, a revolutionary organization of the people of Shanghai in the Qing dynasty. The Dagger Society staged an armed uprising (the first in Shanghai) against the Qing government in response to the formation of the Taiping "heavenly kingdom." Yu Yuan itself was built some 400 years ago. The Pagoda of Lunghua Temple, another of Shanghai's ancient monuments, is said to have been built in the Period of the Three Kingdoms (220–280).

Shanghai is the terminal of Changjiang River shipping lines. It is connected by rail with the north and south of the country, and has lines of communication linking it with all other parts of China, as well as oceangoing ships and international air flights arriving and leaving every day.

In the sea to the east of the province of Fujian there are some eighty islands, big and small, including Taiwan—the smallest of China's provinces but the largest of its islands. Situated between the temperate and the tropical zones, Taiwan has a long summer and no winter. Trees and grass are evergreen, and the people harvest their crops three times a year. Sugar cane and bananas are everywhere to be seen. Taiwan is a beautiful island where "frost and snow are never seen, and flowers blossom throughout the year." The original inhabitants of Taiwan were of Gaoshan (Kaoshan) nationality; they now account for only 3% of the population, most of them living in the mountain areas. The Gaoshan people love singing and dancing, especially at harvest times, and the famous Chu Yue (pestle music) of the Gaoshans incorporates one of the parts of their everyday life—the use of a long stick to pestle rice.

The relation between the peoples to either side of the Taiwan straits began long ago. During the Period of the Three Kingdoms Sun Quan (182–252), the king of Wu, sent the generals Wei Wen and Zhuge Zhi with a large fleet to the island, and during the Sui dynasty people from the mainland again migrated in great numbers to Taiwan, where they cultivated the land and developed Taiwan's economy together with the local inhabitants. From then on, the turbulent Taiwan straits were no longer an obstacle, and economic contacts between the people of Taiwan and the southeastern coastal areas became frequent and close. In the mid-fourteenth century, the Yuan government set up an administrative bureau in the Peng Hu Islands and exercised sovereignty over Taiwan. Toward the end of the Ming dynasty, General Zhen Chenggong (1624–1662) drove the Dutch out of Taiwan, and by 1683 the Qing government had integrated Taiwan politically with the mainland. For nearly a thousand years the people of various nationalities in Taiwan have worked together, fought together against foreign invaders, and together transformed the desolate plains and mountains into a prosperous island, producing rice, sugar, tea, fish, salt, and fruit in large quantities. Near the end of the nineteenth century Taiwan was occupied by the Japanese, who remained until the defeat of Japan in 1945

69

70

69. *The River Huangpu is a branch of the Changjiang (the Yangtze) in its lower reaches. It flows through the city of Shanghai, and near its mouth is broad and deep enough to provide berths for big seagoing vessels.*

70/71. *Street scenes.*

发展体育运动 增强人民体质

72

73

72. *Shanghai Gymnasium, built in 1974. Its arena has a seating capacity of more than 18,000. Many international contests have been held here, as well as concerts and performances of dancing, acrobatics, etc.*

73. *Workers, staff workers, and old people practicing taijiquan (Chinese boxing).*

74. *The building in Shanghai in which the Communist Party of China held its First National Congress on July 1, 1921.*

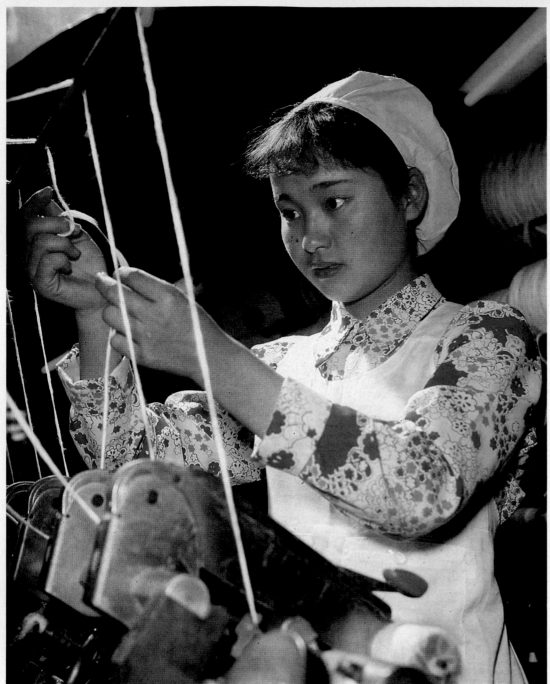

75

76

75. *A young textile worker. Shanghai's textile industry is the most important in China, with 420,000 workers. More and more young people are becoming skilled textile workers.*

76. *Young people enjoying their midday break in a park in Shanghai.*

77. *Actresses backstage in a Shanghai theater.*

78

78. *Dianchun Tang (the Hall for Summoning the Spring). This was the headquarters of the Dagger Society, a secret organization in Shanghai, during the 1853 uprising. Under the leadership of Liu Lichuan the society captured Shanghai and persisted in its struggle against the Qing rulers and foreign invaders for eighteen months.*

79. *Yu Yuan (the Garden of Leisurely Happiness) in Shanghai. Dating from 1559–1577, it has been restored since the Revolution. The picture shows Yangshan Tang (the Building That Looks Up at the Hills), which combines the architectural styles of the Ming and Qing dynasties.*

80. *Tripod red pottery jug. A relic of the later neolithic age, about 4,000 years ago. It was excavated from the lower floor of an ancient site at Dingling, near Shanghai, and was used for cooking.*

81. *Colored pottery urn, of a kind much used by the people of the later neolithic age. It is an example of the Machang-type pottery of the Yangshao culture, known for its red and black lines and beautiful geometrical designs.*

82. *Zhihu (pot with handle) from the reign of the Emperor Xuan Zhong (1426–1435) of the Ming dynasty. This kind of porcelain, in which the colored design is painted on before the application of a pale blue glaze, began to appear during the thirteenth century. The zhihu was not an article for daily use, but rather a sacrificial vessel.*

81

82

83. *You (an ancient high-quality small-mouthed wine vessel) made for the Emperor Fu Ding of the later period of the Shang dynasty (ca. 1600–1122 B.C.). It was a sacrificial vessel, used only by aristocrats, intended to hold aromatic wine to be offered to gods and ancestors during sacrificial rites. Inscriptions were cast inside the you and its lid.*

84. *Gong (an ancient wine vessel made of horn) made for the Emperor Fu Yi of the later period of the Shang dynasty. The front end of its lid bears the image of a monstrous animal with horns like a giraffe, the back end the head of a buffalo. The body of the vessel bears the design of a phoenix.*

83

84

85

86

86. *Watching the sunrise on Tan Hai Shi (the Rock That Stretches Forward to the Sea) on Mount Tai, province of Shandong. Mount Tai, 1,524 m. (5,029 ft.) high, is the first of the Five Sacred Mountains of China. Its many beautiful sights include Nan Tian Men (the South Gate to Heaven), Ri Guan Feng (the Sun Watching Peak), Jingshi Gu (the Sutra Stone Valley), and Heliong Tan (the Black Dragon Pool).*

87. *Mount Tai, province of Shandong. From Daizhong Fang (the Mount Tai Archway) to Nan Tian Men (the South Gate to Heaven) there is a long flight of stone steps. This is the only way to the summit.*

88. *Bixia Ci (the Temple of the Azure Cloud) at the summit of Mount Tai. This magnificent group of buildings dates from the Song dynasty (960–1279). It is reached by way of Nan Tian Men (the South Gate to Heaven), Baiyun Dong (the Cave of the White Cloud), and Lianhua Feng (the Lotus Flower Peak).*

89

89. *The Taishan Temple at the foot of Mount Tai. Here the emperors through the centuries worshipped Mount Tai and prayed to heaven. It is considered one of China's three greatest ancient buildings (the others being the Hall of Supreme Harmony in Beijing's Forbidden City and the Confucian Temple in the county of Qufu, not far from Mount Tai). There are many interesting relics in the temple.*

90. *Stone on Mount Tai, with the inscription "This mountain is the most sacred of the Five Sacred Mountains of China."*

91. *In front of the Apricot Tree Forum, where Confucius used to teach, there is a stone monument set up in memory of the Chinese juniper tree which he planted there.*

90

91

92

93

94

92. *Yan Sheng Kong Fu (the Residence of the Duke Who Spreads Wisdom). In 1055 the Emperor Ren Zhong of the Northern Song dynasty named the forty-sixth-generation direct descendant of Confucius Yan Sheng Kong (the Duke Who Spreads Wisdom) and built a mansion for him which is now usually called the House of the Confucian Family. The buildings were renovated and enlarged to their present size in 1503; there are a total 463 of them.*

93. *The Dacheng Hall, the most important building of the Confucian Temple and the main hall for the offering of sacrifice to Confucius. It was named Dacheng (Complete Achievements) by Emperor Chong Zhong of the Song dynasty in 1104. It was renovated in 1499 by Emperor Xiao Zhong of the Ming.*

94. *The ten stone pillars which support the front eaves of the Dacheng Hall, built in 1499, during the reign of the Emperor Ziao Zhong, and restored in 1724. Each pillar is carved with a relief of two dragons playing with pearls.*

95

96

95. *The old cypress in the Taishan Temple. It is said to have been planted about 100 A.D., during the Han dynasty, and is growing well.*

96. *Entrance to the Confucian Gardens. The gardens form the graveyard of Confucius and his descendants. They contain more than 20,000 old trees and over 1,000 stone tablets, and are surrounded by a wall 7 km. (4.4 mi.) long.*

97. *Wan Gu Chang Chun Fang (the Everlasting Archway), on the road to the Confucian Gardens. It was built in 1594, during the reign of the Emperor Sheng Zhong of the Ming dynasty.*

98

98/99. *Qian Fo Yan (the Cliff of a Thousand Buddhas) at the eastern foot of Mount Haihu (White Tiger Mountain), Jinan, in the province of Shandong. The precipice is 62 m. (205 ft.) high, and 210 statues in it are wonderful examples of the art of stone carving in the early Tang dynasty (618–907).*

100. *The Liao Chamber, where Pu Songling (1640–1715), a famous writer of the Qing dynasty, wrote his* Strange Tales from the Liao Chamber. *Drawing on folk tales widely known among the masses, Songling produced stories about foxes and ghosts, which at the same time exposed the evils of the society in which he lived, and described with particular sympathy the sincerity of young love.*

101. *Fisherman harvesting kelp.*

100

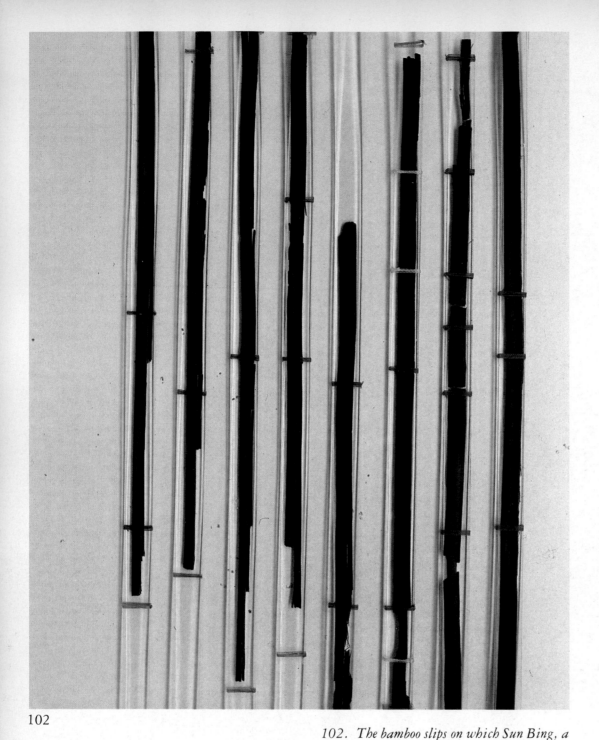

102

102. *The bamboo slips on which Sun Bing, a distinguished strategist of the Warring States Period (475–221 B.C.), annotated his military strategy and tactics. The slips were discovered in April 1972 in a Western Han tomb in the Yinque Mountains, near Linyi in the province of Shandong, after being lost for over 2,000 years.*

103. *Mount Laoshan, to the east of Qingdao, in the province of Shandong. Bordering on the sea, with steep, high cliffs, strangely shaped rocks, and crystal-clear springs and streams, it is a justly famous summer resort.*

104

104. Bringing home the bride—an ancient tradition which still lingers on in the rural areas of Shandong. Here the young husband drives his wife to his mother's house, where they will live.

105. Old people of a people's commune at Weifang, province of Shandong, enjoy the leisure of their remaining years.

106. *Lake Taihu. Situated in southern Jiangsu, with an area of 2,213 sq. km. (860 sq. mi.), Taihu is the fourth largest fresh-water lake in China. It is the center of the network of waterways to the south of the River Changjiang, of the greatest importance for irrigation and water traffic.*

105

107

107. *A stone kylin (Chinese unicorn) standing in front of the tomb of the Emperor Wen Di (560–567) of the Chen dynasty in the Period of the Southern and Northern Dynasties.*

108. *Hall without Pillars in Linggu Temple, Nanjing. The hall is 22 m. (72.6 ft.) high, 58.8 m. (194 ft.) long, and 37.85 m. (124.9 ft.) wide. Built only of brick and stone, it is a masterpiece of architectural design.*

109

110

111

109. The mausoleum of Dr. Sun Yat-sen, who died in 1925. Situated at the foot of the Purple and Gold Mountain, the mausoleum has a solemn and dignified aspect.

110. The Purple and Gold Mountain Observatory. Besides having its modern astronomical instruments, the observatory preserves a collection of ancient Chinese astronomical instruments, including an armillary sphere, an ancient Chinese sundial, an altazimuth, etc.

111. Hu Qiu Hill (Tiger Hill), to the northwest of Suzhou. It is said that He Lu, king of Wu during the Spring and Autumn Period, was buried here. The Ju Qiu Pagoda was built in 959, entirely of brick.

112. The famous Changjiang Bridge at Nanjing, which spans the great river at its lower reaches. The lower-deck railway bridge is 6,772 m. (22,347 ft.) in length, the main bridge 1,577 m. (5,204 ft.). Designed and built by the Chinese themselves, it links the northern and southern communication arteries and has played an important role in promoting economic development.

113

115

113. *Statue of Jian Zhen (688–763), a head monk of the Da Ming Temple during the Tang dynasty, who later crossed the sea to Japan and founded there a Buddhist sect of strict asceticism. Made for the 1,200th anniversary of Jian Zhen's death, the statue stands in the Fa Jin Temple (formerly Da Ming), Yangzhou.*

114. *Arhat statues in the Purple and Gold Shrine in the Eastern Dongting Mountains, 40 km. (25 mi.) from Suzhou. There are altogether sixteen Arhat statues, all just over a meter (3.3 ft.) in height. They are the works of the famous Southern Song dynasty sculptors Lei Chao and his wife.*

115. *The Thin West Lake, Yangzhou, owes its name to its narrow and tortuous shape and its fame to its exquisite and beautiful scenery.*

116. *Suzhou, "the Venice of the East." A view of the main canal.*

117. *Water chestnut is tender and delicious. It grows in large quantities in Lake Taihu, in the vicinity of Suzhou and Wuxi.*

118

118/119. *Mount Huang. Situated in southern Anhui, the mountain is formed of granite, and boasts seventy-two named peaks. It is famous for its rare pine trees, grotesque rocks, seas of clouds, and hot springs.*

120. *Mount Jiuhua, in the county of Qingyang, province of Anhui. This is one of the great mountains of Buddhism in China. It has nine peaks with shapes like lotus flowers, hence the name Jiuhua (Nine Flowers).*

121. *The famous Temple of Zhi Yuan (the Garden of Paying Respects) on Mount Jiuhua. Ancient temples were built in great numbers on the mountain; fifty-six are well preserved today and between them contain some 6,000 statues of the Buddha.*

122

122. *The statue of Yue Fei, an army commander under the Song dynasty (960–1279), in the main hall of the temple in his honor at Hangzhou. Golden-helmeted, golden-armored, and dressed in a purple robe, the national hero radiates health and vigor.*

123. *Statue of Tatagata Buddha, at the center of the Grand Altar in Linying Temple, Hangzhou. The temple was built in 326, during the reign of the Emperor Cheng Di (325–343) of the Eastern Jin dynasty. The Grand Altar Hall is 33.6 m. (110.9 ft.) high, the statue 24.8 m. (81.8 ft.). Famous beauty spots around the temple include the Feilai Feng (the Peak That Comes Flying from the Sky) and Leng Quan (Cold Springs).*

124

124. *The Guo Qing Temple at the northern foot of Mount Tiantai (the Heavenly Platform). The temple was built in 598 during the Sui dynasty. Mount Tiantai is the birthplace of the Tiantai faction of Buddhism, and its high, steep peaks and majestic and beautiful scenery have made it a popular attraction for sightseers.*

125. *A cabinet with traced designs in gold. It was made in the Northern Song dynasty (960–1127), and discovered in 1966 in the Huiguang Pagoda in Xianyan Temple, province of Zhejiang.*

125

126. *Liuhe Pagoda (the Pagoda of Six Harmonies) stands on the slopes of Mount Yuelun (Moon Wheel Mountain) beside the River Qiantang. It was built in 970, during the reign of the Emperor Tai Zhu of the Northern Song dynasty.*

127. *The teahouse at Ping Hu Qiu Yue (Autumn Moon on the West Lake), one of the beauty spots of the West Lake.*

126

127

128. Longjing, a famous green tea, is produced from tea plants on the mountain slopes in the neighborhood of Longjing (Dragon Well), Hangzhou.

129. Silk parasols, not only practical but also objects of beauty, are one of the traditional handicrafts of Hangzhou.

130. The Temple of King Yu. King Yu was a legendary king of China some 4,000 years ago. It is said that he was so busy with his work on water control that he passed by the door of his own house three times without noticing it. The tomb of this great water-control expert—the Great Yu mausoleum—is at the foot of Mount Guizi in the province of Zhejiang. The temple, which stands beside it, was built in 545, during the reign of the Emperor Wu Di of the Southern Liang dynasty, as a memorial to King Yu, and contains many stone tablets erected by later emperors praising his activities.

131. Huangyan, in the province of Zhejiang, is a famous mandarin-orange-producing area. When time to pick the oranges comes around, the whole area presents a vast panorama of color and lively activity.

132. Colored relief of a beast called the Monster of Avarice (now extinct) on the walls of the Temple of King Yu.

132

133

133. *Zhoushan fishing ground, the largest of the Chinese fishing grounds. Lying to the east of the province of Zhejiang, it runs from the Shengsi archipelago in the north to the Taizhou archipelago in the south, and from the Donghai (East China) Sea in the east to the Gulf of Hangzhou in the west. Within it are more than 530 islands, large and small; the biggest, Zhoushan (Boat Mountain), owes its name to its shape, which is like that of a boat.*

134

134. *Sending bamboo rafts down the river, a very common scene in the mountain areas of Zhejiang.*

135. *The Stone Shoot in Xiandu, province of Zhejiang. The mountains here are full of grotesquely shaped rocks, like this one which owes its name to a fancied resemblance to a bamboo shoot.*

136

136. The Putuo Mountains, in the province of Zhejiang, which have been called "a Buddhist kingdom at the end of the earth."

137. The Sanwei (Think Thrice of the Morals in the Books You Have Read) Study, Shaoxing, in the province of Zhejiang. The great Chinese contemporary writer Lu Xun, a native of Shaoxing, studied here when he was a boy. He was the standard bearer of the Chinese cultural revolution, and is the author of the novel An Authorized Biography of Ah Q and others.

138. The East Lake in Shaoxing, province of Zhejiang. Since the Han dynasty this has been used as a stone quarry, producing grotesque precipices and sheer cliffs. Centuries of digging and chiseling lie behind the formation of the East Lake.

139

139. *The Jinjiang Mountains in western Jiangxi. These form part of the Lo Xiao range. The many valleys are surrounded on all sides by high and precipitous peaks. During the second period of the revolutionary civil war, Mao Zedong established a revolutionary base area here.*

140. *An underglazed green porcelain plate from the Yuan dynasty, produced 600 to 700 years ago in Jingdezhen, province of Jianqxi. Jingdezhen, known as "the porcelain capital," has played an important role in the history of Chinese porcelain.*

140

141. *Longtou (Dragon Head) Rock, also called She Sheng (Suicide) Rock. This famous beauty spot commands a view of Lake Poyang, the largest fresh-water lake in China.*

142

142. The twin pagodas in Kai Yuan Temple, Quanzhou, province of Fujian. Quanzhou was described by Marco Polo in 1298 (then it was called Zayton) as one of two biggest ports in the world, the other being Alexandria in Egypt. The pagoda to the east, 48.24 m. (159.2 ft.) high, is the Zheng Guo Pagoda (the Pagoda That Guards the Country); it was built in 805 in the Tang dynasty. That on the west, 44.06 m. (145.4 ft.) high, is called Ren Shou (the Pagoda of Benevolence and Longevity) and was built in 916, during the Liang dynasty of the Period of the Five Dynasties. The 160 statues of Buddha's

warrior attendants, deities, Arhats, knights, and Bodhisattvas in relief are among the finest examples of ancient Chinese sculptural art.

143. The Green Peak, also called the Fairy Damsel Peak, at the head of Er Qu Creek, in the Wuyi Mountains, province of Fujian. The mountains are of red sandstone and are not very high, averaging 600 m. (1,980 ft.) above sea level.

145

144. *Riyue Tan (the Lake of the Sun and Moon), a natural lake in the province of Taiwan. The lake is divided into Ri Tan (the Sun Lake) and Yue Tan (the Moon Lake) and is 722 m. (2,383 ft.) abope sea level, with an area of 4.4 sq. km. (1.7 sq. mi.).*

145. *A group of Gaoshan people of Taiwan, one of China's many ethnic minorities and the earliest inhabitants of Taiwan. They live in the mountain areas. Agriculture is their main occupation, but they also hunt and fish and have many crafts—knitting, weaving, artistic carving, etc.*

Chapter V   Central and South China—Zhongnan

1. The ancient culture of Zhongzhou

2. The land of Chu

3. Guangdong, gateway to the south

4. Guiling leads the world in beauty

The region of Zhongnan lies in the central and southern part of China. It neighbors Huabei in the north, Huadong in the east, and Xinan in the west, and is washed by the South China Sea along its southern coastline. It consists of the four provinces of Henan (Honan), Hubei (Hupeh), Hunan, and Guangdong (Kwangtung) and the Guangxi (Zhuang) Autonomous Region, formerly Kwangsi Province. It covers an area of more than a million square kilometers (390,000 sq. mi.) and has a population that exceeds 200 million. To the south lies the vast expanse of China's territorial waters, dotted with archipelagos—the Dongsha Islands, the Xisha Islands, the Zhongsha Islands, the Nansha Islands—spread like pearls over the South China Sea. Zengmu Ansha of the Nansha Islands, about latitude 40° North, constitutes the southernmost tip of China's territory.

1. The ancient culture of Zhongzhou

Four thousand years ago China was divided into nine administrative divisions, of which the central division, Yu Zhou, was the present-day province of Henan. The terrain of Henan slopes down from west to east, with the Xiao and Funiu Mountains sprawling at its western edges, the Tongbo and Dabie Mountains along its southern border, and the Taihan Mountains in the north.

The ancient Chinese fable of "The Foolish Old Man Who Removed the Mountains" is a tale of the Taihan Mountains. Long, long ago there lived a Foolish Old Man. As there were two great peaks, Taihan and Wang Wu, standing in front of his house and obstructing the way, the Foolish Old Man made up his mind to remove them, he called his sons to help and set about digging up the mountains with great determination. When God saw this, he was so moved that he sent down two angels, who carried the mountains away on their backs. This fable has become a household story among the Chinese, and the tale of the Foolish Old Man has acquired, with the years, a practical application as an example of steadfastness and unremitting effort.

In the center of Henan stands Mount Song, one of the Five Sacred Mountains of China. On its southern slope is the site of an academy of classical learning by the name of Songyang, whose building is now more than 1,000 years old, and at the foot of the mountain is the Shaolin Temple, the original home of the famous school of Chinese boxing known as Shaolin Quan. The vast Nanyang basin flanks the Funiu Mountains in the south, and to the east stretch the boundless plains of the Rivers Huanghe (the Yellow River) and Hueihe, which, under intensive irrigation, have become an important region for growing wheat, peanuts, cotton, and tobacco. The Huanghe crosses the northern part of the province. In the gorge between the Zhongtiao and Xiao Mountains, its passage is blocked by two lone islets, aptly called in Chinese "the tide-stemming pillars in midstream," where the fast-moving waters, shooting headlong through the narrow passage, form the three great rapids that give the gorge its present-day name of San Men (the Three Gates). After the liberation of the people of Henan, perhaps inspired by the memory of the Foolish Old Man, determined to change nature, and, blowing up the midstream islets, constructed a great dam in their place. Ten immense reservoirs have also been built in the middle reaches of the Hueihe, and the harnessed waters of the two rivers have brought great benefit to the descendants of the people who settled this ancient land of Zhongzhou.

Zhongzhou played an outstanding role in the history of China, and it is here that the curtain first lifted on China's ancient culture. At Yangshao Village, in the county of Mianchi, archeologists have discovered the site of an ancient village dating back to the later part of the neolithic age more than 6,000 years ago. An enormous number of stone and bone tools, as well as much pottery, were found here—among them bone arrowheads used for hunting, stone hoes for farming, stone spinning wheels, bone needles for weaving, and pottery vessels for holding water and grain. These finds, and the archeological data associated with them, are usually lumped together under the name "the Yangshao culture."

Almost 3,500 years ago China instituted its first slave state under the Shang dynasty, with its capital, Yin, in the north of Henan, about 3 km. (1.9 mi.) from the present-day town of Anyang. Here, at the small village of Xiaotun, the ruins of Yin have now been unearthed. Over 10,000 artifacts were found on the site, among them some famous characters carved on tortoise shells and bones; these are China's earliest recorded writing, used to chronicle what our ancestors had learned about astronomy, the calendar, meteorology, and the techniques of production. There are also a number of pieces of bronze tableware, implements for sacrificial ceremonies, and a magnificent bronze square din (a four-legged incense burner) by the name of Simuwu, decorated on all sides with patterns of coiled dragons and Taotie (a legendary man-eating beast), and weighing no less than 875 kg. (1,900 lb.).

Another ancient capital in this part of Henan is the town of Luoyang, famous for nearly 1,700 years as "the capital of nine dynasties." The construction of a city here was begun by Prince Jidan of Zhou as early as 1108 B.C., but the actual capital of Zhou remained at Xian until 770 B.C. From this date Luoyang served as an imperial base during the Eastern Zhou, the Eastern Han, the Wei part of the Three Kingdoms Period, the Western Jin, the Northern Wei, the Sui, and the Tang. The White Horse Temple to the east of the city is China's first Buddhist temple, originally built in 68 A.D. To the south lies Longmeng Hill, also known as Yique Hill, the site of the world-famous Longmeng grottoes, which date back to the Northern Wei period 1,500 years ago. Here over 90,000 Buddhist statues of all sizes have been carved out of the cliff walls of the hill, the tallest measuring 17 m. (56 ft.) in height, and as many as 1,352 Buddhist caves have been gouged out of the rock. The place is often known as Thousand Buddha Caves.

Yet another of China's ancient capitals is Kaifeng, traditionally known as Bianliang or Bianjing, in the north of Henan. Prince Hui of Wei, in the Warring States Period, set up his capital here some 2,300 years ago, and subsequently Kaifeng was capital during the Period of the Five Dynasties, for the Later Liang, the Later Jin, the Later Han, and the Later Zhou, and

then for the Northern Song. The Xianguo Temple in Kaifeng dates from the sixth century, and Longting (the Dragon Pavilion) is a fine example of the palace architecture of the Northern Song period.

2. The land of Chu

The provinces of Hubei and Hunan, in the middle of Zhongnan, were the territory of the state of Chu during the Warring States Period. Hubei lies to the north of Lake Dongting, bordered on the west by the Wushan, Lingshan, and Wudang Mountains, overgrown with luxuriant primeval forests and rising to between 2,000 and 3,000 m. (between 6,600 and 9,900 ft.) above sea level. Its central area is formed by the Jianghan plains and criss-crossed by the Changjiang (Yangtze) and Hansui Rivers and their tributaries, and there is more high country to the east.

The Changjiang enters Hubei from the west and, after tumbling through a narrow cleavage in the Wushan Mountains, feathers out to form the Three Gorges, often called "the throat of the Yangtze." Just as the Rhine in Europe is inseparable from the myth of the Lorelei, so the Three Gorges are associated with the legend of the Goddess of Mount Wushan, and the peak named after her is shrouded throughout the year in mist and floating clouds. The towering rock faces of the Three Gorges, so high that they often keep the sun off the river until after midday, and the fantastic scenery of this famous stretch of water offer one of the most fascinating river trips to be made in China. After the Three Gorges, the waters of the Changjiang settle down to a gentler progress across the Jianghan plains. In the past, during the high water between summer and autumn, if the surging body of water was not diverted in time, the river would overflow and flood the surrounding area with calamitous results. After the liberation a flood-diversion dam was built here, and thus the threat to the country on either bank was averted. A large water-control center was also built by the people's government in the middle reaches of the River Hansui, so that this too has now been harnessed for navigation, power generation, and the irrigation of the surrounding country.

Wuhan is the capital of Hubei. The city area is divided by the Rivers Changjiang and Hansui into three parts—Wuchang, Hanyang, and Hankou. At this point the Changjiang is guarded by two hills—Gueishan and Seahan (the Tortoise and the Snake Hills)—which face one another from either bank like two eternal sentinels, and the main railway line from Beijing to Guangzhou crosses the bridge across the Changjiang and runs straight on into Guangdong. Wuhan is again one of China's ancient cities, with a history that stretches back 3,000 years to a time when, as the town of Ezhon, it was the fief of Prince Hong, son of Xiongqu, king of Chu. During the Period of the Three Kingdoms, Hankou was already an important meeting point for water and land communications.

The terrain of Hunan, the province to the south of the Dongting Lake, climbs steadily from north to south. The Nanling Mountains in the south form the watershed between the Changjiang and Pearl Rivers, and are rich in such nonferrous metals as tungsten, antimony, lead, and zinc. To the

west, the Wulin and Xuefeng Mountains produce tung trees yielding the tung oil that has earned a great reputation at home and abroad. Beyond the Xiangjiang River towers Mount Heng, the southernmost of the Five Sacred Mountains of China.

The northern part of the province of Hunan is formed by the low, flat Dongting plains with the enormous Lake Dongting at the center. Lake Dongting, 250 km. (156 mi.) in circumference, is the second largest fresh-water lake in China, and the area surrounding it is criss-crossed by dense networks of waterways; this is famous as a plentiful land of fish and rice. Standing majestically by the side of the lake, the thousand-year-old Yueyang Tower, to the west of the city of Yueyang, was built in the Tang dynasty and later refurbished in the Song. Fan Zhong Yan, a man of letters of the Northern Song dynasty, wrote truly of the sublime magnificence of Lake Dongting in his *Record of the Yueyang Tower:* "Rimmed by distant mountains and fed by the Changjiang, vast and mighty, the waters of the lake sweep to infinity."

To the south of Lake Dongting and on the lower reaches of the Xiangjiang River is Changsha, a city with a history of more than 2,000 years. It is here that the prince of Changsha was given his fief in the early years of the Han dynasty, and in 1972 a female mummy was unearthed at Mawanguui, which was later identified as that of a noble lady of the Han dynasty. Today Changsha is the political, economic, and cultural center of the province of Hunan, where Mao Zedong carried out the revolutionary activities of his early years. Shaoshan, in the county of Lin, near Changsha, was the birthplace of Mao Zedong.

In 1965 a large-scale irrigation system was built at Shaoshan, and a wide area of farmland profited as a result; as part of this system, an aqueduct dubbed "the Shaoshan Milky Way" was installed across the River Lienshi, a tributary of the Changjiang.

There is a small river to the north of Changsha called the Miluo, which has always had a special significance for the Chinese, for it was here that China's great poet and patriot Qu Yuan drowned himself in 278 B.C. This was a time when Chu was the victim of repeated aggression by the neighboring state of Qin, and had suffered one defeat after another. Qu Yuan offered many suggestions to the king of Chu with a view to strengthening his country, but all of them were rejected. In great distress and bitterness, he gave vent to his pent-up feelings in the long poem *Li Sao (Sorrowful Complaint),* which later became extremely famous, and drowned himself in angry protest. Every year on May 5 of the lunar calendar, the day of Qu Yuan's suicide, the people commemorated the death of China's first major poet and threw boiled zongzi (pyramid-shaped dumplings made of rice wrapped in reed leaves) into the Miluo to lure the fish away from the poet's body. Thus racing dragon boats and eating zongzi have come down from the past as the traditional customs for the festival in memory of Qu Yuan.

3. Guangdong, gateway to the south

The province of Guangdong is a coastal province and China's gateway to the South China Sea. Across the province runs the Pearl River, which flows into

the sea through the Pearl delta, an area famous for its grain, silk, and tropical fruit.

Of the offshore islands the largest is the island of Hainan, with the five peaks of Mount Wuzhi towering above it like the five fingers of its name. Lying in the tropical zone, the island has a tropical atmosphere and is rich in tropical fruit, coconut palms, litchis, longans, bananas, pineapples, oranges, tangerines, and lemons as well as in such industrial crops as rubber, sugar cane, and sisal hemp. Of the peninsulas along the coast the largest is the Leizhou Peninsula, on the eastern side of which is Zhanjiang, an important port built after the liberation for the development of foreign trade in South China.

Twenty-five hundred years ago Guangdong was under the influence of Chu, the state which then covered both Hunan and Hubei, and ever since the succeeding Qin dynasty Guangdong has been one of China's administrative divisions and the gateway to the south. The people of Guangdong are courageous, hardworking, and above all adventurous. From earliest times there have never lacked brave spirits who confronted the sea and traveled far away to the Malay Archipelago, the Malay Peninsula, and Indonesia, either in search of agricultural employment or to engage in industry and trade. Today, Chinese of Guangdong origin can be found almost all over the world.

The island of Hainan is the home of several hundred thousand descendants of the ancient Beiyue minority. These are the Li people, a national group of brave, hardworking people especially characterized by their love of freedom. March 3 of the lunar calendar is their traditional festival, when boys and girls walk in groups out of the villages and in passionate singing and dancing pour out their love and choose their lifelong partners.

Guangzhou (Canton), the capital of Guangdong, is the largest city in South China, with a population of 2 million. According to legend there were once five celestial beings in dresses of different colors who, riding five goats as colorful as their costumes, came to the city and made the local people a present of some rice stems, each of which contained six ears of grain. In order to keep alive the memory of this visitation, the people of Guangzhou built a temple called Wuxian (the Temple of the Five Celestial Beings), and Guangzhou is also known as Wuyang (the City of Five Goats), or just Yang—Goat City. Since China was unified in the Qin dynasty, Guangzhou has gradually become the main center of politics, the economy, and culture in South China; it has a port for foreign trade in Wangpu harbor, in its eastern suburb, capable of accommodating oceangoing ships. China's Spring and Autumn Export Fairs have been held annually in Guangzhou since 1957, and the Guangzhou International Trade Center was set up here in 1979.

Guangzhou has also been the scene of many achievements of the Chinese people in their struggle against imperialism and feudalism during the last two centuries. In 1840 Lin Zhexu, one of the national heroes of China, burned stocks of opium illegally imported into the country by British merchants. In 1911 the members of the revolutionary parties staged an uprising in which more than 100 of them sacrificed their lives at

Huanghuagang—an important step in the progress toward the declaration of the republic by Dr. Sun Yatsen later the same year. In the middle twenties Guangzhou was once again a cradle of revolution, for it was here that Mao Zedong set up the Peasant Movement Institute, the site of which is still preserved, and it was here too that the Army of the Northern Expedition received the order to march against the warlords.

Since the Revolution great changes have taken place in Guangzhou, and it now is not only a center of light industries, such as sugar refinery, paper making and textiles, but also is well developed in iron and steel making, and machine building. Yet Guangzhou is still a beautiful city, famous for its green vegetation all the year round, and for its festive flower fairs, teahouses, and restaurants which serve delicious dishes of snakemeat and other Cantonese delicacies. A well-known sanatorium, the Conghua Hot Spring, is 81 km. (50 mi.) away.

4. Guiling leads the world in beauty

In ancient times the district of Guangxi belonged to the Beiyue people. Emperor Qin Shi Huang, founder of the Qin dynasty, three times sent troops to quell the Beiyues and, when at last he succeeded, set up prefectures in the region. In order to facilitate communications and the movement of troops, a canal was dug which linked the Xiangjiang and Lijiang Rivers; named Lin Qu (the Soul's Channel), this was the earliest canal built in China.

Guangxi is inhabited today by such minority peoples as the Zhuang, the Miao, and the Yao, with the Zhuang numbering about 7 million. This autonomous region is the area of China most heavily settled by minority groups. Like their Han compatriots, the Zhuang are a fearless people who will not give in to oppression. Significantly, the Taiping "heavenly kingdom" movement during the Qing dynasty originated here: led by the peasant revolutionary leader Hong Xiuquan, it aimed to establish a "heavenly empire of great peace," but was suppressed, with French and British help, by the Manchu emperor in 1864.

The Zhuang love singing. It is their custom to hold a Ge Wei (a free-for-all singing contest) regularly every year, when boys and girls get together in matchmaking by singing love songs. The legendary figure Sister Liu III was such a songster who made her name during the Tang dynasty. Today there is a saying, "Thanks to the sweet voice of Sister Liu III, Guangxi is a sea of song."

Guangxi is mostly hilly country, with limestone accounting for more than half the geological structure of the area. Because of the high average temperature and rainfall, this soft rock is especially subject to erosion, which, in turn, explains the fantastic nature of the karst scenery in this area. The whole region not only is characterized by green hills and clear streams, but abounds in grotesquely shaped hills, rocks, and caves.

Guiling, situated on the River Lijiang, is one of the most famous beauty spots in our country. The entire town is overgrown with more than a hundred thousand osmanthus trees, thus making it literally an osmanthus forest, or Guiling in Chinese. Every year in midautumn the trees burst into blossom and drown the city in a flood of intoxicating fragrance. Places of special beauty within the city boundaries include Dashiu Peak (the Peak of Solitary Beauty), Elephant Trunk Hill, the Seven Star Rock, the Reed Flute Rock, and the Fig Tree Lake. The River Lijiang meanders among them like a silken belt and weaves them into a gorgeous tableau of infinite variety. As the old folk saying goes, "The fantastic peaks grow like a jasper forest; the blue waters ripple like silken gauze." At Reed Flute Rock to the northwest of the city, there is a cave gouged out of the cliff wall whose main chamber can accommodate a thousand people at a time; its ceiling and floor bristle with stalactites, stalagmites, stone pillars, stone drapes, and even stone flowers, all in shapes as fantastic as can be imagined, and the walls are adorned with so many strange figures—some like waterfalls, some like roaring lions—that people call the chamber "the art gallery of Mother Nature." Take a pleasure boat down the River Lijiang to Yangshuo, where you will find a cluster of peaks rising sheer out of the water and spaced in the design of a lotus blossom. Gliding over the crystal-clear surface of the Lijiang past the imposing Green Lotus Peak, you will chant with the ancients:

Guiling leads the world in beauty,
But Yangshuo is supreme in Guiling:
Peaks and streams vie with one another in splendor,
But each without the others is nothing.

146. *The statue of Buddha Lushena at Fengxian Temple, 17.14 m. (56.6 ft.) in height.*

147

148

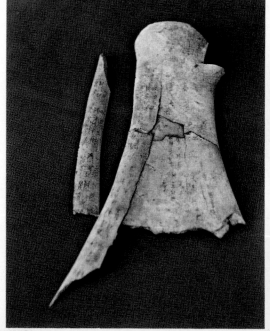

149

198

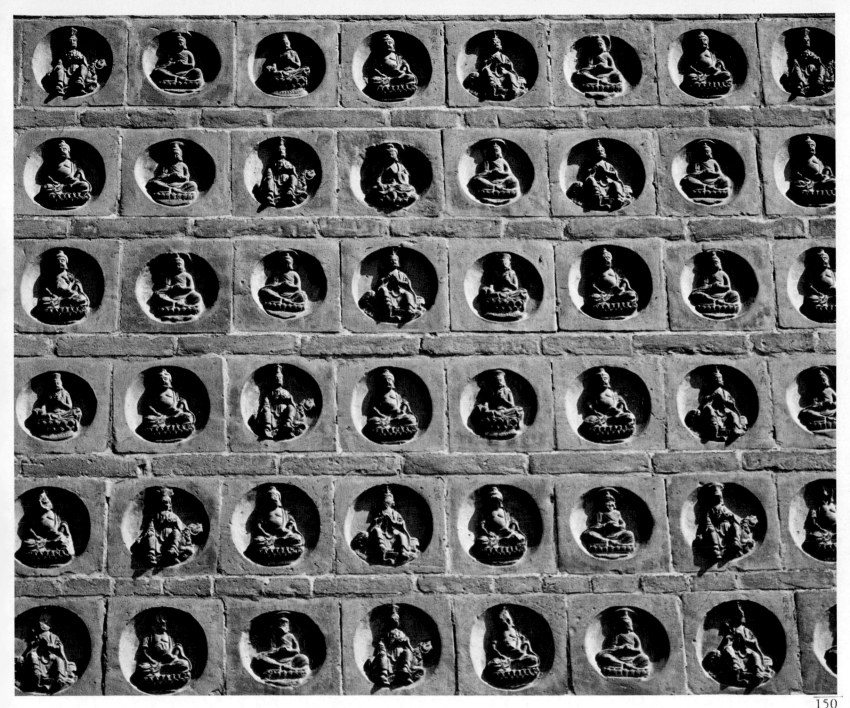

147. *Detail of the Iron Pagoda at Kaifeng.*

150. *Details of the Yueyang Tower.*

148. *The Iron Pagoda at Kaifeng, constructed during the Northern Song dynasty (960–1127). It is octagonal in shape and thirteen stories (54.66 m, or 180.4 ft.) high. The outer wall is inlaid with glazed bricks in twenty-eight different shades of brown, to form ornamental designs such as flying Apsaras, kylins (unicorns), Buddhas, monks, and flowers.*

151. *A lively scene from the Bie embroidery at Kaifeng, province of Henan. Although it is about 1,000 years old, this exquisite embroidery still retains its clear depth of field, vividness, and verisimilitude. This panel is based on a famous painting of the Song dynasty, "A River Scene at Qing Ming."*

149. *Tortoise-shell and bone inscriptions of the Zhou dynasty. They were first discovered at the ruins of Yin in the county of Anyang, province of Henan, in 1899. Out of 4,500 characters that have so far been identified on shells and bones only about 1,700 have yielded their meanings.*

152

153

152. *Pagoda tombs in the Shaoling Temple in the county of Denfeng, province of Henan. Built in the fifth century, the temple is flanked on the east and west by pagoda yards. The one on the west side contained about 220 pagoda tombs, hence its name, Taling (the Pagoda Forest). When a monk of the temple dies, his remains are assigned to a pagoda tomb whose height and number of stories correspond to his Buddhist learning and position.*

153. *A scene in the Taihangshan Mountains, west of the plains of Hebei. In these regions life still preserves many of its old characteristics: here the peasants are spreading wheat to dry in the sun.*

154. *The Red Flag Channel in the province of Henan. This water-control project, which involved the hewing of 1,500 km. (940 mi.) of channel out of sheer granite cliffs, was undertaken by the people of Henan to bring the waters of the River Zhang to the county of Ling.*

155

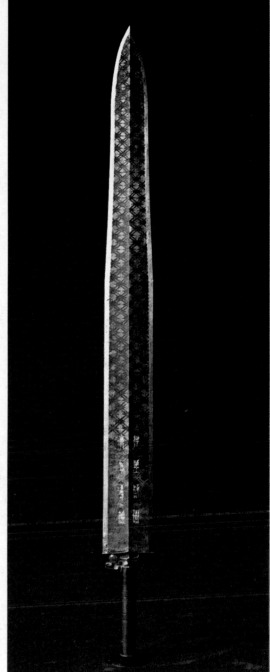

156

155. Located to the east of Wuhan in the province of Hubei, the East Lake is five times the size of the West Lake of Hangzhou.

157

156. Bronze sword unearthed in 1965 at the site of Yin Du, the ancient capital of Chu, in what is now the province of Hubei. On the upper part of the blade, in Wu Zhuan (seal characters), are inscribed the words "This sword was made and used by Goujian, King of Yue." Goujian ruled from 496 to 465 B.C.

157. Statue of the patriotic poet Qu Yuan, who drowned himself in 278 B.C., in front of Xingyin Ge (the Poem Chanting Pavilion) on the East Lake.

158

160

159

158. *The River Liuyanghe in the eastern part of the province of Hunan. A tributary of the Xiangjiang, the Liuyanghe follows a twisting course for most of its 217 km. (135.6 mi.). The popular song "Liuyanghe" is a convincing evocation of the landscapes along its banks.*

159. *The Yueyang Tower by the side of Lake Dongtin. It was built in the Tang dynasty, about a thousand years ago. In his* Record of the Yueyang Tower *Fan Zhong Yan, a scholar of the Song dynasty, wrote of it, "From the glory of the morning sun to the glow of the evening twilight, the tower is blessed with a thousand changing views."*

160. *Shaoshan, the birthplace of Mao Zedong, where he spent his childhood.*

161

162

161. The Martyrs' Tomb at Huanghuagang. Sun Zhongshan (Dr. Sun Yat-sen), Huang Xin, and their comrades, in their bid to overthrow the Qing dynasty, prepared an attack on Guangzhou before launching the northern expedition, but the plan leaked out and met with failure. More than a hundred revolutionaries died as a result. Seventy-two bodies were collected later on and interred at Huanghuagang. The uprising shook the whole nation, and served as a prelude to the Wuchang uprising which was to topple the feudal rule in China for good.

162. Porcelain statue of the Mitao Buddha, from Shiwanzheng in the city of Fushan. Fushan is one of the four great cities of China, and Shiwanzheng is famous for its pottery and porcelain. The Mitao Buddha is a deity much loved by the people.

163. The Temple of Zu: details of the decoration.

163

164

166

164. Mother and son from the province of Guangdong.

165. Dragon-boat racing, held every year on May 5 to commemorate the great patriotic poet Qu Yuan of Chu, who committed suicide out of bitterness and anger against the helplessness of the ruler of Chu in the face of foreign aggression.

166. Every year 12 million babies are born in China, but the future for Chinese children is now very different from what it was 100 years ago.

165

167

169

168

167. Village life in Guangdong. Although China is fast catching up with the rest of the world in industrial output, more than 80% of the people still live on the land and the old skills are still important.

168. The whole of Chinese agriculture depends on the system of irrigation, much of it still in use after more than 2,000 years.

169. A fisherman catching shrimps.

213

170

170. *Longtan Feipu (the Dragon Pool beneath a Cliffside Waterfall), in the Dinbu Mountains of Guangdong.*

171. *Fishing and salt industries are well developed on the island of Hainan. Here there is a community for the Li and Miao peoples, under the jurisdiction of the Autonomous Region of Hainan.*

172. *Rock formations on the coast of Hainan. In ancient times, when the first visitors from the mainland landed on the uninhabited island of Hainan, they must have thought they had come to the end of the world. Maybe this is why it is also called "a pillar in south heaven."*

173. *View between tropical palms on the island of Hainan. With an area of 32,200 sq. km. (12,400 sq. mi.) Hainan is second in size only to Taiwan among China's coastal islands.*

174. *Terraced fields built by the hardworking people of the various ethnic groups in the Guangxi Autonomous Region. The scarcity of cultivable land has encouraged the populations in the hill regions of China to terrace and irrigate every available square meter of their terrain.*

171

175

176

175/176. *Views of Guiling, in the Autonomous Region of Guangxi. The city is famous for the beauty of its setting in the surrounding countryside.*

177. *The pavilion at the top of Mingyue Peak (the Peak of the Bright Moon), on Mount Diecaishan (the Multicolored Mountain) to the north of Guiling. The pavilion, high above the surrounding country, offers magnificent views over the city of Guiling.*

178. *Silk-ribbon dance by Zhao Qing, a famous dancer. This type of dance, in which two silk scarves are combined with the coordinated movements of the arms and body to create plastic forms literally out of thin air, has been studied and performed for many years.*

179. *The unique landscapes of Guiling owe their origin to the karst topography of the region. The River Lijiang is lined on both banks by fantastically shaped hills, and boating on the river in this scene produces a strange sense of unreality.*

180/181. *The Lijiang meanders among the razor-sharp peaks of Guiling. It is 83 km. (51.9 mi.) from Guiling to Yangshuo by boat, and there is a surprise for the tourist at every bend of the river.*

182. *Underwater fisherman with harpoon in the Guangxi countryside.*

Chapter VI Southwest China—Xinan

1. The land of abundance

2. The road of the Long March

3. A mosaic of nationalities

4. The roof of the world

The region of Xinan consists of the provinces of Sichuan (Szechwan), Guizhou (Kweichow), and Yunnan and Xizang (Tibet), which is now an autonomous region. It covers an area of approximately 2,310,000 sq. km. (900,000 sq. mi.—one-quarter of the whole of China) and has a population of more than 100 million; most of China's national minority groups live in this region. Topographically it is very varied, with a changeable climate: the Qinghai-Xizang (Tibetan) plateau, famous as "the roof of the world," the Yungui plateau with its "10,000 crags and torrents," and the Sichuan basin, called "the land of abundance," are all within its territory. Here are fertile plains, boundless grasslands, dense forests, rich mineral resources, immense hydroelectric potential, and all kinds of rare and valuable wild animals.

1. The land of abundance

The province of Sichuan (Four Rivers), so called because of the four great rivers which flow through it—the Changjiang (the Yangtze), the Minjiang, the Tuojiang, and the Jialingjiang—was developed early in the history of China. More than 2,000 years ago, in the Spring and Autumn Period and the Warring States Period, people were already farming this fertile land and had built irrigation systems here. At that time Sichuan was divided into the two states of Ba and Shu; Ba occupied the eastern part of the Sichuan basin, around Chongqing (Chungking), and Shu the western part of the basin in the area of Chengdu. Both states were eventually conquered by the forerunners of the Qin dynasty, who annexed their territory and set up a prefecture in the region. Later Zhuge Liang (181–234 A.D.), the celebrated statesman and strategist, urged Liu Bei (182–252), a member of the royal house of Han, to use the ideal terrain formed by Jinzhou (now part of Hubei and Hunan) and Yizhou (the Sichuan basin) to create a state which would be difficult to attack and strategically well located, with land that was rich and fertile. This became the kingdom of Shu during the Period of the Three Kingdoms, and lasted from 221 to 263. In ancient times the torrential waters of the River Minjiang often overflowed, flooding the plains of Chengdu. To relieve the people of the disastrous floods, Li Bing, the prefect of Shu under the Qin dynasty, and his son, used the ancient art of water control to build an irrigation system that has become famous in Chinese history, the Dujiangyan (the Weirs of the River Du). The weirs were built near the county of Guan, where the Minjiang flows from the mountains into the plains, in 316 B.C., and from that time the Chengdu plains have been free from drought and flood and the region a land of abundance with favorable weather. Li Bing and his son recommended that the weirs should be examined and repaired yearly, the waterways dredged regularly, and more weirs built in the lowlands—and this system has now been in operation for over 2,200 years, effectively irrigating large fertile areas of the Chengdu plains. The Er Wan Temple (the Temple of the Two Kings) was erected in honor of Li Bing and his son, and still stands majestically on a hill near Dujiangyan. After the establishment of the new China, the government enlarged this ancient irrigation system enormously, and the area has become one of China's main rice-producing districts.

There are more than eighty rivers in Sichuan. The Changjiang pours down into the province from the Qinghai-Xizang plateau, and flows out of it through the Hunan-Hubei basin to Shanghai and the sea. It is 6,300 km. (3,900 mi.) long and the third longest river in the world, after the Nile and the Amazon; its drainage area covers 1,920,000 sq. km. (740,000 sq. mi.) with a population of more than 300 million people. It traverses the entire province of Sichuan, joined on the way by its tributaries the Minjiang, the Jialingjiang, the Tuojiang, and the Ujiang, and flows through much mountainous country, forming rocky gorges with many rapids and shoals. On its way through the eastern part of Sichuan it is suddenly narrowed by the Wushan and Wulingshan Mountains, and surges into the famous Three Gorges on the border of Sichuan and Hubei. The Changjiang (Yangtze) Gorges, cut deep into the limestone rock, with walls towering sometimes thousands of feet into the sky, are spectacular and dangerous. The depth of the water and the irregularities of the river bed make the surface rough, with swirling whirlpools, and only recently has the river here been made safe for shipping. As you thread your way by river steamer, tall mountains rise precipitously along either bank and huge rocks, appearing suddenly in front of your boat, seem to bar the way; but just as you think you can proceed no further, behold, the clouds disperse and a rock disappears just as suddenly as it came, and there before you an entirely different rocky scene unfolds. The famous Tang dynasty poet Li Bai has left an evocative picture of the gorges in his day:

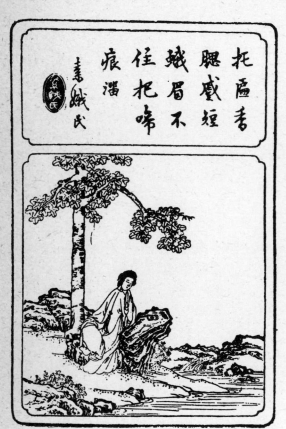

In the bright clouds of dawn I leave Baidicheng,
A thousand li to Jiangling take only a day;
I hear the cries of monkeys on the banks,
As my light boat passes through the folds of countless hills.

Chengdu, in the center of the Chengdu plains, is the capital of the province of Sichuan. This ancient city was built in 316 B.C. by the Qin rulers in the latter part of the Warring States Period; since then it has been the political, economic, and military center of the southwestern region of China. It became the capital of the kingdom of Shu in the Three Kingdoms Periods, and during the Tang dynasty was considered one of China's four most important cities, the others being Changan, Handan, and Fangzhou. During the Eastern Han dynasty Chengdu became known for its brocade and was thus called "the brocade City," and later, in the Period of the Five Dynasties (907–960), the king planted lotuses all over the town, so that it became known also as "the lotus city"; it is still called Rong (Lotus) for short. In the southern suburbs stands the Wu Hou Memorial Temple, in honor of Zhu Ge Liang, the prime minister of Shu in the Three Kingdoms Period, who was made Baron of Wu by the king. The temple stands solemn and dignified among old and towering trees in the magnificent temple grounds; in front of the statue of Zhuge Liang are three copper drums more than a thousand years old. The ruins of the Shan Pavilion, where the famous poet of the Tang dynasty Du Fu once lived, lie in the western suburb of Chengdu. On these ruins the Du Fu Straw Pavilion, and the Du Gongbu Memorial Temple (in memory of Gongbu, an important government official) have been built to honor these two eminent men.

Leshan is another ancient city, south of Chengdu, with a history going back more than 1,300 years. Outside the town stands the famous Giant Buddha of Leshan, carved out of the Lingyun cliffs in the Leshan Mountains. This huge Buddha, 70 m. (231 ft.) high, sits upright with its back against a giant rock, watching over the broad expanse of water where the Sichuan, the Dadu, the Minjiang, and Qingyi Rivers meet. Here the currents are swift and treacherous, and the statue was built, at the instigation, it is said, of the monk Hai Tong, to protect boatmen from disaster. Work on it began in 713 and continued through most of the eighth century; it is China's largest Buddha in the open. To the west of Leshan is Mount Emei. It is 3,094 m. (10,210 ft.) high, and looks westward to the Daxue and Gongga Mountains in the far distance.

Chongqing (Chungking), built on the side of a mountain, is the largest industrial and commercial city in the Xinan region, and also its largest river port; from this point one can travel up the Changjiang to Yibing or downstream to Wuhan, Nanjing, and Shanghai. It is also the place at which the Chengdu-Chongqing, the Sichuan-Guizhou, and the Siangyang-Chongqing railways converge, and is therefore the hub of the land and water communications of the region. Surrounded by mountains and rivers, Chongqing sparkles at night when the lights from the houses on the mountain slopes join with the galaxy of stars in the sky. Chongqing is not only a historic city but also the site of many of the revolutionary struggles of the more recent past. It was here, during the war against Japanese aggression, that Zhou Enlai and many other revolutionaries fought some of their toughest battles. A museum has now been built at Red Crag Village, Zhou Enlai's home at that time, in his honor.

2. The road of the Long March

The Long March of the Chinese Red Army in 1934 and 1935 was the most glorious single chapter of the Revolution.

This was a period of great hardship and suffering in China. The first Communist base had been established in the province of Jiangxi in 1927, and in the following year the Chinese Red Army of Workers and Peasants was created under the leadership of Mao Zedong and Zhu De. During the years from 1930 to 1934 the Red Army was under constant attack from the Kuomintang forces of General Chiang Kai-shek, and eventually its leaders determined to evacuate their original base and march north to a strategically sounder position in the mountainous country of the northern part of the province of Shaanxi.

They set off in October 1934, marched along the Nan Mountains, and reached Guizhou early in January 1935. Taking advantage of the rugged, hilly country of southwest China, they crossed the Yunnan-Guizhou

plateau and the majestic Wumeng Mountains on the Yunnan-Guizhou border, and turned northward into southern Sichuan, where the headwaters of the Changjiang, the Shujiang, the Yuanjiang, and their many tributaries cut into the plateau like swords, digging out deep gullies and gorges and making the uneven surface of the terrain more hazardous still. To the west of Sichuan lie the Hengduan Mountains, with their high snow-covered peaks and deep valleys: here the River Jinshajiang rushes south between the Shaluli and Ningjing ranges, through the Grand Canyon to the northeast of Shigu, with its Tiger Leap Gorge, known all over China. Fighting and outwitting the Kuomintang army at every turn, twisting and redoubling on their tracks, they slogged and struggled through uninhabited regions and across the territory of semisavage tribes, where they were sometimes hard put to find a guide to keep them on their route. In the course of almost exactly a year they crossed twenty-four rivers and eighteen mountain chains, captured sixty cities, and tramped wearily across endless stretches of desolate grassland, covering a total of 12,500 km. (7,800 mi.). Of the 90,000 who set out, only 20,000 reached their destination in the north of Shaanxi. It was an epic expedition that has been called far more difficult than Hannibal's crossing of the Alps.

Nor was it undertaken, like Hannibal's expedition, by a body of trained soldiers with efficient equipment. These were really workers and peasants, typical Chinese people of their period, ill shod and ill clothed, who carried with them on the backs of donkeys everything that they needed for the building or repairing of bridges, for the making of ammunition and weapons, footwear and clothing. By their achievement they kept alive the flame of revolution at a critical moment in modern Chinese history, and even fanned it into a blaze in the many regions through which they passed. It was a huge step, not only in the creation of the People's Republic of today but in the consolidation of that brotherhood of the various Chinese nationalities that has become one of its chief characteristics.

3. A mosaic of nationalities

Of the thirty or more minority groups living in the Xinan region, the Zang (Tibetan), the Miao, the Yi, the Bouyi (Puyi), the Dai (Thai), the Hui, the Hani, and the Bai (Pai) have the largest population. Yunnan has the most minority groups of any Chinese province; the minorities in Guizhou account for a large proportion of its population. The whole region of Xinan, including the Autonomous Region of Xizang (Tibet), inhabited by the Zang people, can be considered a mosaic of China's great family of nationalities.

The ruling class of old China adopted a policy of racial discrimination and oppression toward the minority groups. The valiant, industrious people of the groups in the southwest led a poor and miserable existence, and there were conflicts and feuds between them. After the new China was established, the Communist government adopted a policy toward the minority groups which ended this dark era in their history; now, together with the Han people, they have become the masters of their country, with their own autonomous regions, prefectures, and counties.

Due to historical, environmental, and religious differences, the customs and habits of the southwest minority groups contrast with those of the northwest region. The Miao live mainly in the valley of the River Qingshuijiang (the River of Clear Water) and in the Miao Mountains, where on special occasions such as marriages and funerals the music of reed pipes can be heard ringing across the hills. They have many kinds of sporting and leisure activities, such as bull fights and dragon-boat races. The Miao women are renowned for their embroidery, producing beautiful and exquisite work, without any premeditated design. The minority youth express their feelings of love in various ways. The Dong sing to their lovers in the moonlight; the Mia perform the traditional ritual of the Yao Ma Lang (Shaking the Rider on Horseback); the tradition of the Shui people is to sing, dance, and beat copper drums at their festivals. During their annual Water Sprinkling Festival, the Dai people dress in their colorful national costumes, sing and dance, have dragon-boat races and rocket contests, and enjoy themselves splashing water on each other. A grand trade fair is also held at this time. An even grander trade fair is held annually on the fifteenth day of the third moon of the Chinese lunar calendar. On this day the Bai, Li, Hui, Miao, Dai, and Naxi (Nahsi) people come to Dali for the fair, bringing cattle, horses, monkeys, mules, medicinal potions, and other local products, and enjoy a variety of colorful leisure and sporting activities. The southwest region is rich in forests and exotic wildlife. In the western part of Sichuan, the northwest part of Yunnan, and the southwestern part of Xizang, there is a large forest zone second only to that in the northeast region of China. There are many varieties of tropical plants in this area as well as fig, mahogany, teak, and Chinese cypress trees; the trees of the temperate zone include pine, Chinese fir, cypress, birch, maple, nanmu, camphor, and elm; in the colder areas there are dragon spruce, fir, and Yunnan pine trees. In Xishuang Banna, in the province of Yunnan, the Dai people live in small communities where vast rubber plantations, several hundred different species of medicinal plants, and a hundred or so species of oil-bearing plants are to be found, and also rare animals like Asian elephants, rhinoceroses, green peacocks, and gibbons. In the remote thickly forested mountain areas of Sichuan too there are many wild animals including oxen, antelope, golden monkey, and musk deer, as well as the very rare and much-loved giant panda. And in the mountains of Guizhou there are tigers, leopards, wolves, foxes, and squirrels—so that the region of Xinan fully deserves to be called, as it is, both "the green jewel" and "paradise for animals."

Kunming, the provincial capital of Yunnan, is a "city of spring" with springlike weather the whole year round. The coldest month of the year is January, when the temperature averages 9.8°C. (49.6°F.); in July, the hottest month of the year, the thermometer is not likely to go above 20°C. (68°F.).

Lake Dianchi, or Lake Kunming as it is sometimes called, lies in the lower part of the city. The main places of historical and cultural interest are the

Huating Temple, the Taihua Temple, the Sanqing Pavilion, and the Lungmen stone inscriptions. Near Mount Biji (the Blue Cock Mountain) lies the tomb of Ne Er, a famous Chinese musician and the composer of the national anthem of the People's Republic. The Stone Forest is situated at Lunan, on the slopes of the red-earthed hills; the peaks and trees in this district have taken on many strange shapes, some resembling swords piercing the blue sky, others like lotus blossoms, or old men and graceful ladies. These unusual natural forms make an impressive and charming sight.

4. The roof of the world

The Qinghai-Xizang plateau in the southwest of China is the highest and largest plateau in the world. It averages about 4,500 m. (14,900 ft.) above sea level, and has often been called "the roof of the world." The Autonomous Region of Xizang, with an area of 1,200,000 sq. km. (460,000 sq. mi.) forms the principal part of the plateau. To the north are the snow-covered Kunlun Mountains; in the center are the rolling Tanggula Mountains, and in the south lie the Gandisi and Himalayas. The Himalayas stretch in an unbroken chain across the southwestern part of Xizan, along the borders of China, Pakistan, India, Nepal, Sikkim, and Bhutan, a total length of more than 2,400 km. (1,500 mi.). Qomolongma Feng (as the Chinese call Mount Everest), on the Sino-Nepalese border, is the highest peak in the Himalayas as well as in the world. Vast, undulating uplands stretch the length of the Xizang plateau, and there are some 1,500 lakes scattered over the area, with herbaceous vegetation growing in abundance on their shores. Their waters yield many valuable industrial chemicals, such as borax, Xizang nitre, and salt. The southeastern mountain areas of the plateau are covered with large expanses of dense virgin forest, inhabited by monkeys, river deer, black bears, pandas, and lynx.

The Zang people (the Tibetans) form an important part of China's great family of nationalities. Friendship between the Zang and the Han people dates back to ancient times. Early in the Warring States Period the Han people had developed close contact with the Zang tribes living in the province of Sichuan, and during the Tang dynasty the Tang rulers did a great deal to promote the relationship between the two peoples. In particular, they allowed intermarriage, and in the year 641 the Emperor Tai Zhong of the Tang dynasty betrothed the Princess Wen Cheng, a daughter of the royal house, to Songzan Ganbu, the zanpu, or ruler of Tufan (the name of Xizang at that time). Princess Wen Cheng's marriage to the Tibetan ruler has been through the centuries a symbol of unity between the Han and Zang people.

Before the establishment of new China, the Zang people had been exploited for many years, and even the old tradition of friendship between the Han and Zang people had been destroyed. Xizang was peacefully liberated in 1951, and since 1959 the people's government has abolished serfdom and carried out many democratic reforms in the region. Thus the Zangs have leaped from feudalism to socialism and their country has undergone tremendous changes in the last twenty-five years. In the past Xizang had no industry of its own, and the Zang people could not produce even the simplest object; since 1956 about 250 factories have been set up, among which the woolen mill in Linzhi is an ambitious enterprise with modern equipment. In the old days, there were practically no highways in the region, just narrow winding tracks only passable by horses and cattle; now a network of 1,580 km. (988 mi.) of highways has been built. Originally, in the vocabulary of the Zang language there were no words meaning "workers," "industry," or "machine," but today among the workers and technicians in the Xizang factories 80% are Zang people. The communes in the region have modern farm machinery and tractors. The Zang people have opened up mountains, built canals and ditches, planted trees to extend the forest areas, built dams and reservoirs. Culture and education have flourished too. Two institutes of higher education and many secondary schools have been set up. There are more than 4,000 primary schools in the rural areas. Before the liberation, the Mengba and Lhoba people in Xizang didn't have their own script; they wrote by carving signs on wood or tying knots in ropes. Now some of their young people are university students. The capital of the Xizang region is the legendary city of Lhasa. It is situated on the north bank of the River Lhasa, a branch of the River Yarlung Zangbu, and lies more than 3,600 m. (11,900 ft.) above sea level, where the air is thin and the sun shines for twelve hours a day. It has been called "the sunlight city." The most famous building in Lhasa is the Potala Palace to the west of the town. This magnificent structure, thirteen stories and 100 m. high, stands majestically on Mount Hongshan (the Red Mountain). It was for centuries the traditional seat of the Dalai Lama. Its construction is said to have been started by Songzan Ganbu in the year 650, and it was renovated and extended by the fifth Dalai Lama in the seventeenth century. In its present form it is more than 300 m. (990 ft.) long and over 100,000 sq. m. (24 acres) in area. The outer walls are made of granite, and inside them are mansions, temples, palace buildings, and fortifications.

The roof of the main palace is covered with copper tiles; it is surrounded by eight large sacrificial halls, each having at its center, an exquisite golden pagoda inlaid with all kinds of precious stones. Inside the palace, carved pillars stand in great numbers, and long corridors cross and recross one another. The walls are literally covered with colored murals depicting all kinds of historical and many other subjects. Lhasa is one of China's most ancient cities, and one of its most fascinating. The name Lhasa means "the holy city" in the Zang language, and until about twenty-five years ago nearly a quarter of the adult males in Tibet were Buddhist monks, or lamas, living in 2,500 monasteries spread about the country. In Lhasa's Da Zhao Temple and the Xiao Zhao Temple many cultural relics from the Tang dynasty have been preserved, symbols of the close link between Xizang and the Chinese people that has existed since ancient times.

183. *The Giant Buddha of Leshan is one of China's largest stone Buddhas. The figure is 70 m. (231 ft.) high, with shoulders 28 m. (92 ft.) wide and fingers 8.3 m. (27.4 ft.) long. The head alone is 14.7 by 10 m. (48.5 by 33 ft.) and is covered with 1,021 curls. The space between its feet can seat more than 100 people. According to legend, a Tang dynasty monk of Lingyun Temple named Hai Tong was concerned that this spot, where the waters of three rivers converge in a treacherous confusion of currents, was a hazard to boatmen, and had the idea of carving a statue of the Buddha to protect them. Work on it was begun in 713 and continued for most of the eighth century.*

184

184. *Wu Gorge, the longest of the Changjiang (Yangtze) Gorges. Wu Gorge is 40 km. (25 mi.) long and over 1,000 m. (3,300 ft.) above sea level. The famous twelve peaks of the Wushan Mountains tower to either side of the river, Mount Goddess the most spectacular among them. Song Yu, a poet of the state of Chu in the Warring States Period, described how King Xiang of Chu (298–264 B.C.) dreamed that he had an audience with the Goddess, who told him that whenever she went abroad, if she went in the morning it brought mists, if in the evening, rain would come.*

185. *Jiu Zhai Channel (the Channel of the Nine Stockaded Villages). The channel owes its name to the nine ancient Zang villages in the vicinity. The main branch is more than 60 km. (37.5 mi.) long, and 108 lakes are spread around it like emeralds inlaid in the mountains. It was called the Emerald Sea in the past.*

186

187

188

186/187. *The world-famous giant panda lives only in the remote mountains of northwest Sichuan. The giant panda is gentle in disposition, and its movements are sluggish. It feeds on crisp, sweet bamboo and occasional birds or other small animals such as snakes and squirrels.*

188. *The statue of the Buddha Puxian in Wan Nian Temple (the Temple of 10,000 Years) on Mount Emei. Begun in 980 during the reign of the Emperor Tai Zhong of the Northern Song dynasty, it is 7.4 m. (24.4 ft.) high. The bronze elephant weighs approximately 62 tons.*

189. *The halo of Buddha on the top of Mount Emei (Omei). This phenomenon, visible from Jindin Peak (Golden Top), occurs on still days when the sun shines again after rain. Looking at the halo, a spectator can sometimes see his own shadow reflected in thin air.*

190

190. *Wind-instrument player at the traditional Torch Festival of the Yi people. This takes place in the "Tiger Month" of the Yi calendar (July in the Western year). There are many festival activities, rich in the folk traditions of the Yi people.*

191. *Girls of the Yi people. Some 700,000 Yi people live in their own communities in the Liangshan Yi Autonomous Prefecture in the southwestern part of the province of Sichuan. Before the Revolution serf systems prevailed here, but today the wooden plough and hoe and the stone farming implements of those days have given way to modern farming techniques; the former serfs are rebuilding their own native land.*

192. *The new masters of the grasslands return after pasturing cattle and sheep.*

193. *The Stone Forest in the province of Yunnan. These fantastic stone pillars, from 20 to 40 m. (from 66 to 132 ft.) high, are formed by the corrosion of layers of limestone.*

191

194. *A stockaded village of the Blangs (Pulang). The Blang people number more than 40,000. They are an ethnic group with a long history. Living in the mountain areas around the middle and lower reaches of the Lancangjiang River in southwest Yunnan, they farm in hilly country and cultivate plantations.*

195

194

195. *The Dai (Tai) people celebrating the Water Sprinkling Festival. Held every year in the sixth or seventh moon of the Dai calendar (mid-April in the Western calendar), this is a traditional Dai festival. According to legend it is the birthday of Buddha, and the people splash or sprinkle water at each other, wish one another good luck and happiness, hold dragon-boat races, and, of course, worship the Buddha. By this celebration they hope to avoid the illnesses and sufferings of the past year and ensure that the coming year will bring them abundant harvests, more livestock, and increased prosperity.*

196. Mural in the Potala depicting the life of the Zang people. On the walls in the Potala are large numbers of murals, some as high as 5 m. (16.5 ft.), some tens of meters long. Apart from their artistic value, they contain a vast amount of valuable historical detail.

197. The Temple of Za Shi Lun Bu, situated at the foot of Mount Niseri within the domain of the city of Rikaze. Built in 1447, during the reign of the Emperor Yin Zhong of the Ming dynasty, the temple contains many ancient cultural relics.

198/199. Princess Wen Cheng, a daughter of the royal house of the Emperor Tai Zhong of the Tang dynasty. She was betrothed to Songzan Ganbu, the ruler of Tufan, now Xizang. She brought with her to Tufan the advanced techniques of the Han people for the making of pottery, paper making, wine brewing, etc., and so made great contributions to the economic and cultural life of the country. The mural in picture 198 shows the scene of her entry into Xizang. Picture 199 shows a statue of the princess.

200. The Potala Palace, Lhasa, in the Autonomous Region of Xizang. Standing majestically on Mount Hongshan (the Red Mountain), it was for centuries the traditional seat of the Dalai Lama, and is one of the most famous buildings in China. Legend has it that Songzan Ganbu, the zanpu (head) of Tufan (the ancient name of Xizang), began the building of this palace in the seventh century. It was enlarged into its present form in the seventeenth century by the fifth Dalai Lama.

197

198

199

201

201. Lamas (Buddhist monks) in the Temple of Zhebang (the Wise Clam) in the western suburbs of Lhasa, where the third and fifth Dalais once resided. Only twenty-five years ago or so nearly a quarter of the adult males in Tibet were lamas, living in 2,500 monasteries.

202. De Yang Mansion, in the Potala, built half way up a hill, 70 m. (230 ft.) and more above the ground. The courtyard in front of the mansion has an area of 1,600 sq. m. (17,800 sq. ft.). In the past, during festivals, this was used for the staging of dramas and dances to exorcise evil spirits and entertain the Dalai Lama.

203. People of Lhasa enjoying a traditional Zang drama in Chongsaikang Square to celebrate the Zang New Year. This is a traditional festival observed most ceremoniously by the Zang people, who gather together to exchange good wishes, drink highland barley wine and buttered tea, perform Zang dramas, and dance to the music of the xianzi, a three-stringed plucked instrument.

204. Qomolongma Feng, on the Sino-Nepalese border. Better known in the Western world as Mount Everest, this is the highest peak of the world's highest mountain range, the Himalayas. Qomolongma means "Goddess No. 3" in the Zang language. The mountain is 8,848.13 m. (29,198.8 ft.) above sea level, and is ice-capped all through the year.

202

203

205

205. *Yaks on the pasturelands of the Xizang plateau. Having strong, solid hoofs, they can carry heavy loads in the thin air of the high mountain ridges. They are known as "the ships of the plateau."*

206. *Zang people providing a tea break for the Chinese Revolutionary Army.*

207. *A column of Chinese cavalry guarding the furthest borders of Xizang.*

1. The ancient city of Xian

2. The home of the Revolution, Yanan

3. The Silk Road

4. The frontier

The region of Northwest China is the great hinterland of China. Its eastern and southeastern districts are formed of loess plateaus and the Qinling Mountains. In the southwest is the Qinghai plateau, in the northwest the Gansu Corridor and the great basins to either side of the Tianshan Mountains. Northwest China's northern and western districts have frontiers with the U.S.S.R., Mongolia, Afghanistan, and Pakistan. It consists of three provinces—Shaanxi (Shensi), Gansu (Kansu), and Qinghai (Tsinghai)—and the Autonomous Regions of Xinjiang (Uygur) and Ningxia (Hui). Xinjiang was once Sinkiang Province, and Ningxia was once Ningsia Province. Northwest China is thinly populated. It has an area of more than 2,940,000 sq. km. (1,100,000 sq. mi.), one-third of the total area of China, but a population of about 45 million that only makes up one-twentieth of the country's total. Apart from the Han people there are Uygur, Hui, Tibetan, Kazak, Mongolian, Kirgiz, Ozbek, Yugur, Xibe, Tartar, and Tajik nationalities spread about the various districts, among them Lamaists as well as other Buddhists and a great many moslems. Most parts of the northwest are more than 1,000 m. (3,300 ft.) above sea level—some parts of it very much more—and it is quite different from the other regions in scenery, climate, ethnic composition, and local customs. Here are steep mountain ridges, snow-covered peaks reaching into the clouds, exuberant grasslands covering enormous prairies, and vast expanses of desert stretching as far as the eye can see. The whole of the northwest has a typical climate: it is dry, with a yearly rainfall in most districts of less than 250 mm. (10 in.). The winter is long, the summer short, and there are great differences in temperature during the day. There is a popular saying, "Wear a fur coat in the morning but a cotton shirt at noon, and in the evening eat melons around a fire." Only in the east, in the province of Shaanxi, do more temperate and fertile conditions prevail.

1. The ancient city of Xian

Xian, formerly called Changan, is the capital of the province of Shaanxi. It is situated in the rich central Shaanxi plain, to the south of the River Weihe and to the north of the Qinling Mountains. From the eleventh century B.C. to the tenth century A.D. it was successively the capital of eleven dynasties, among them the Western Zhou, the Qin, the Western Han, the Sui, and the Tang, and the people in the Lulin and Chimei uprisings at the end of the Han dynasty, and the peasant uprising led by Huang Chao at the end of the Tang dynasty, also made it their political center. From all this Changan can lay claim to being one of the most important cities in Chinese history. The central Shaanxi plain has been a center of habitation and activity for the Chinese since the Stone Age. In 1953, the ruins of a new stone age civilization of 6,000 years ago were discovered in the village of Banpo on the eastern outskirts of Xian. In the 10,000 sq. m. (2.5 acres) already excavated here are the remains of forty-five houses, six pottery kilns, and 250 graves, as well as an enormous collection of working implements and household utensils. The implements are mostly made of stone—such as axes, chisels, knives, shovels, arrowheads, spinning wheels, and millstones—or of bone, such as awls, needles, gigs, and fishing hooks. The household vessels are mostly earthenware, and include examples of the large pottery jars in which children were buried.

In the city of Xian itself there are many reminders of a glorious past. In the eighth century A.D., when Changan was the capital of the Tang dynasty, it was probably the largest city in the world, with a population of over a million. Now, in spite of the enormous industrial development and expansion of modern Xian, parts of the urban area of the Tang city are still green fields. Most interesting, perhaps, of the surviving Tang monuments is the Dayanta Pagoda, built in the seventh century as a part of the Temple of Great Kindness and Gratitude. This temple was designed especially to preserve the Buddhist scriptures brought back to China by the itinerant Buddhist monk Xuan Zhuang, whose journey along the Ganges and into southern India was one of the great travel epics of early Chinese history. The pagoda is 64 m. (211 ft.) high, and built with bricks ground exactly to fit each other, so that after more than a thousand years there is still not the least inclination of the structure. Inside, the pagoda is decorated with linear engravings; at the entrance is a tablet bearing the words "An Introduction to the Buddhist Religion by Tangsanzang." The Forest of Steles was made in the eleventh century to preserve the Kaicheng Scriptures in Stone; in it are kept well over a thousand tablets of various kinds, dating from the Han and Wei dynasties, which provide precious material for the study of Chinese history and for research on the ancient Chinese arts of calligraphy, painting, sculpture, and ornamentation. The belfry and drum tower of Xian date from the fourteenth century (Ming dynasty), but the Huaqing Spa (originally called the Hot Spring Palace) in the southern part of the county of Lintong is another Tang survival. Here the Emperor Li Longji and his imperial concubine Yang Yuhuan took their baths—a fact recorded by the poet Bai Juyi of the Tang dynasty, who wrote that "in Huaqing Spa in the chill of spring, the fountain washed warmly over her cream-like skin."

But all the other historic monuments at Xian pale into insignificance beside the discovery made in 1974 to the east of the city, where the vast man-made hill that houses the tomb of Qin Shi Huang, the founder of the Qin dynasty, rises from the valley of the Weihe. Here members of the Yan Zhai Commune digging a well came across a life-sized pottery figure of a warrior buried upright in the earth 4.8 m. (16 ft.) underground. He proved to be part of a great army of such figures, which included swordsmen, spearmen, archers, and cavalry with chariots and horses, all drawn up in battle array in orderly rows to defend the dead emperor. Many of them bear signs of individual portraiture, and all were probably colored. There are more than 8,000 figures in the three huge pits that have been located—a spectacular memorial to the man who "fought millions with a thousand war chariots" and gave his name to China.

2. The home of the Revolution, Yanan

Yanan is in the northern part of the province of Shaanxi. Standing in the mountainous country on the banks of the River Yanhe, it was a place of strategic importance for the defense of the Shaanxi plains in the Tang and Song periods. Close by tower the peaks of Mount Boatashan (the Mountain with the Precious Pagoda), Mount Phoenix, and Mount Qingliangshan (the Cool Mountain), and the city wall, built with sandstone and loess, winds up from the bank of the river to the summit of Mount Phoenix and links together this curious intermingling of water, city, and hills. On the loess plateau below the town are rows of cave dwellings and on the slopes of the valley tiers of terraced fields: here can be seen the unique phenomenon of people dwelling in caves on the mountainside with carts and horses passing overhead. The Baota Pagoda is a nine-story octagonal building 44 m. (145 ft.) high, built in the Tang dynasty. Since the thirties of our century this pagoda has become famous throughout China as a symbol of the revolution.

In October 1934 Mao Zedon, Zhou Enlai, and Zhu De led the famous Long March of the Red Army of Workers and Peasants, from Jiangxi, and after a journey of 12,500 km. (7,800 mi.) across wild and often uninhabited regions the marchers arrived in this area in October 1935. From this time on the area around Yanan was the home of the Revolution. In 1937 and 1938 the Central Committee of the Chinese Communist Party had its headquarters at the foot of Mount Phoenix; in November 1938 the Central Committee moved to Yangjialin, 3 km. (1.9 mi.) from Yanan. After 1944 the Central Secretarial Offices of the Chinese Communist Party were moved to Zaoyuan, 7 km. (4.4 mi.) from the city; Wangjiaping, not far away, was the original headquarters of the Central Military Committee and the Eighth Route Army. Many combat orders and other orders for the disposition of troops were sent out from here in the days of the revolutionary war.

From 1941 to 1944 in Nanniwan, 45 km. (28.1 mi.) to the south of Yanan, the 359th Brigade of the 120th Division of the Eighth Route Army made a great drive to reclaim the barren land and open it up to cultivation, and after four years of hardship the wilderness was transformed into a "Yangtze valley on the frontier" and became self-sufficient in food and clothing. In the Yanan of today, apart from the preservation of these former sites of revolutionary memory, industry, agriculture, and urban reconstruction have all made big strides forward. The former loess plateau has become a scene of great productive activity.

3. The Silk Road

Since very early times the northwest region has been a thoroughfare for trade and cultural exchange between China and other nations. Though most parts of the region are either plateau or desert, the people of ancient times discovered a long and narrow passage that started from Lanzhou on the east and passed between the mountains that lie to the west of the upper reaches of the River Huanghe (the Yellow River) to Yumenguan. This passage, called the Gansu Corridor or the Hexi Corridor, was the only practicable route to Xinjiang and Central Asia from the interior of China in olden times.

雙目送行雲

As far back as 138 B.C. Zhang Qian, appointed by the Emperor Han Wu Di as emissary to the West, used this route. Starting from Changan, he passed through Yumenguan (northwest of Dunhuang) and along the southern slopes of the Tianshan Mountains, covering a distance of many hundreds of kilometers in a few weeks. Thence he climbed over the Pamirs to Dawan (now Philgana in the U.S.S.R.) and arrived finally at Kangju, better known as Samarkand. On his way back he recrossed the Pamirs and followed the northern slopes of the Kunlun Mountains to Changan. Zhang Qian's mission to the West lasted thirteen years, and he and his companions suffered all kinds of hardships; but they made an essential contribution to the opening of this route to the West. After that, many people traveled westward by it; the monk Fa Xian, of the Eastern Jin, reached India by it, and so did Xuan Zhuang of the Tang dynasty, returning with the Buddhist scriptures that are now housed in the Dayanta Pagoda at Xian. Foreign and Chinese emissaries, scholars, and traveling merchants came and went by this route with increasing frequency. Along it China imported religion, art, colored glaze, and woolen goods from abroad, and exported handicrafts and silk goods in bulk, as well as the techniques of silk reeling, iron smelting, and paper making. According to early Indian documents, Chinese silk and silk goods were already being imported into India in the fourth century B.C., and ancient Greek records show that Chinese silk goods had already found markets in Greece in the third century B.C. The Greeks called China "the silk country," and in time this route that connected China with the West came to be known as the Silk Road. For many centuries the Silk Road still followed, more or less, the routes that had been taken by Zhang Qian. By the Han dynasty these had settled into the southern and northern routes. The former went through Yangguan, Shanshan (now Ruoqiang), and Yutian (now Hetian) and past Aerjinshan, Kunlun, and the northern foot of the Kalakunlun Mountains to Suoche, then over the Pamirs to Dayuedi in the valley of the River Amuhe, thence to the Persian city of Anxi, and finally to Daqin, in the territory of the Roman Empire. The northern route still went through Yumenguan, then to Jiaohe, along the southern slope of the Tianshan Mountains to Guizi (now Kuche), to Shule (now Kashi), and over the Pamirs to Dawan, Anxi, and Kangju.

At one time the Silk Road produced a really flourishing trade. Markets were opened along the way, and many Buddhist shrines were built for the solace of the travelers. Among them are the famous stone caves of Dunhuang, more than 1,600 years old, of which the Mogao Caves of a Thousand Buddhas are the largest. Today there are still 492 caves. The frescoes cover a total area of 4,500 sq. m. (50,000 sq. ft.), and there are more than 2,000 colored carved figures, the biggest 33 m. (109 ft.) high and the smallest only a few centimeters. They are a testimony to the inexhaustible ingenuity of ancient Chinese craftsmen.

Other caves in the province of Gansu include those at Maijishan and the Temple of Bingling. In the Autonomous Region of Xinjiang there are the Kezier Thousand Buddha Caves at Baicheng, the Kubentula Thousand Buddha Caves at Kuche, and the Thousand Buddha Cave at Lake Yaer in

Tulufan. The total number of Buddhist caves in the region amounts to more than 600—astonishing relics of a distant culture, strung out like brilliant pearls of memory along the old Silk Road. A memory of a different kind is evoked by the male and female mummies unearthed from the Niya ruins in Xinjiang. They come from a grave of the Eastern Han dynasty, and the silk garments of the Han period which they wore were still intact at the time of excavation.

4. The frontier

The provinces and autonomous regions of Northwest China cover huge areas and contain many high mountains. The grasslands, however, are fertile and excellent for agriculture and for grazing. As a result, most of these areas are divided between cultivated lands and pasturelands, and are rich in both agricultural produce and livestock. The various nationalities living in this region have depended from time immemorial on agriculture and livestock for their livelihood. In the past, agriculture has been backward, and the raising of livestock has been a primitive operation. Since the inauguration of the new regime thirty years ago, however, the methods of production in agriculture and stock raising have been radically changed. Mechanization has been introduced and productive efficiency raised. At the same time the development of industrial construction has proceeded rapidly. In the Xinjiang (Uygur) and Ningxi (Hui) Autonomous Regions not a matchstick or a nail used to be produced, but now the beginnings of an industrial system have been established. Throughout the northwest steel, electricity, coal, petroleum, machinery, chemical, textile, silk-reeling, sugar, leather, paper, pharmaceutical, and food-processing industries are all being developed. Underground resources like petroleum, coal, and nonferrous and rare metals are beginning to be used, and the completion of the Baotou-Lanzhou and Lanzhou-Xinjiang railways has dramatically reduced the distance between the northwest frontier and the interior. The old Silk Road has been replaced by a network of communications as intricate as a spider's web. There are already many colleges and universities, and primary and secondary schools are common in out-of-the-way mountain villages; agricultural and scientific research organizations have sprung up, and research workers have produced one achievement after another, pushing modernization forward at greater speed.

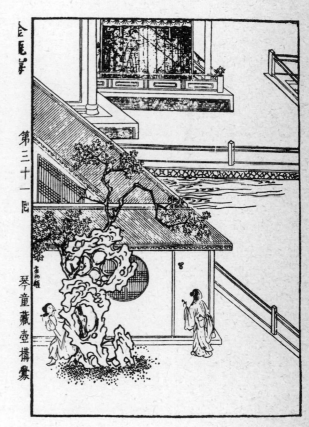

Lake Qinghai, a salt-water lake lies 3,197 m. (10,550 ft.) above sea level. It is the largest lake in China, with an area of 4,427 sq. km. (1,727 sq. mi.). It has an abundant supply of delicious and scaleless fish. Around it is a wide expanse of grassland—excellent natural prairies. To the north is the Chaidamo basin, with rich deposits of petroleum and various metals; it also produces huge quantities of salt. Anyone entering the Ningxia region whose plains extend on either bank of the River Huanghe, sees a whole network of channels and criss-cross footpaths threading between rice fields. This has been a grain-producing area from ancient times. To the west lie the grasslands at the foot of the Helanshan Mountains, where valuable sheepskins are produced.

The Tianshan Mountains tower across Xinjiang for a distance of more than 1,700 km. (1,060 mi.) As the famous border poet Cen Cen wrote, "innumerable the steep peaks covered in snow." The Tianshan range, with its unlimited supply of water, feeds the oases and grasslands both to the north and to the south. At the foot of Mount Bogeda, 1,900 m. (6,300 ft.) above sea level, is a notable beauty spot, Lake Tianchi. Made up entirely of snow waters from the surrounding mountains, it measures 4 km. (2.5 mi.) from north to south and more than 2 km. (1.25 mi.) from east to west. All around it are peaks, snow-covered throughout the year, and on its banks are thick forests of firs; there is serenity and dignity in the reflection of the mountains in the blue waters.

To the north and south of the Tianshan Mountains live thirteen minority nationalities with a total population of 12 million. They differ widely in their customs, costumes, religion. The industrious Uygur people mostly dwell in south Xinjiang and engage in agriculture, while the fierce and tough Kazak people live in north Xinjiang and raise livestock. These two important minority groups are mostly believers in Islam, and there are more than 1,900 mosques in Xinjiang catering to the religious needs of the Moslems.

Xinjiang has always been known as "the land of song and dance." Every Uygur or Kazak, man or woman, young or old, can dance and sing. An old verse vividly describes the style of Uygur dancing: "treading the colored carpet with raised eyebrows and rolling eyes, red sweat drips from the crown of pearls." Anywhere you go to the north or south of the Tianshan Mountains, you can hear the music of the dutaer or the rewafu and watch the graceful and unconstrained dancing of the local people. In the joy of dancing and singing they express their love for their motherland, their joy of living, and their hope of the future.

208. Three-color glazed pottery was widely produced in the early Tang dynasty, and is remarkable for its vividness of design and brilliance of coloring. By the middle of the eighth century its fame had already spread far beyond the ancient city of Changan, and it was being introduced into Japan, Iraq, Syria, Iran, and Russia.

209

209. In March 1974 one of the most astonishing archeological discoveries of the twentieth century was made in the county of Lintong, province of Shaanxi. An entire army of life-sized figures of warriors and horses, buried for over 2,200 years, began to be unearthed in the tomb of Qin Shi Huang, the first emperor of the Qin dynasty (221–207 B.C.). The three pits so far discovered, amounting to a total area of about 20,000 sq. m. (5 acres), contain more than 8,000 figures, standing in battle array in orderly rows, equivalent in number to a guards division. The whole of this fantastic assembly formed part of the burial company of the dead emperor.

210. Figures discovered in the pit of warriors and horses in the tomb of Qin Shi Huang. These were made of clay baked in a kiln and then painted with a variety of colors. The height of a warrior figure varies from 1.78 to 1.87 m. (from 5.87 to 6.17 ft.), and many were obviously intended as individual portraits.

211. A round-mouthed tripod wine vessel of bronze, made in the Zhou dynasty about 3,000 years ago. The body of the vessel is decorated with the faces of animals; the two perching birds are purely ornamental. Wine was warmed over a fire in this vessel.

211

210

212. The Du Tiger Tally was a proof of authority for the movement of troops in the Qin dynasty. Du was the name of a county in the state of Qin, about 4 km. (2.5 mi.) from Xian. The tally is made of copper in the form of a tiger, and consists of two halves, one of which was retained by the emperor and the other by the garrison commander. Only when the two halves were fitted together could troop movements be made.

213. Hua, one of the Five Sacred Mountains of China, lies to the south of the county of Huayang, 120 km. (75 mi.) from Xian. The three principal peaks are the Falling Wild Goose Peak in the south, the Sun Facing Peak in the east, and the Lotus Flower Peak in the west. The three of them are like the three legs of a tripod.

212

214

215

214. *Central view of the Mogao caves.*

215. *The Yangguan Pass on the old Silk Road, by the Gudong Sands at Dunhuang, province of Gansu. The Silk Road, winding through the desolate regions on its way to the West, was for centuries the trade route for the exchange of merchandise between China, the Middle East, and Europe.*

216. *The Mogao caves, now known as the Caves of a Thousand Buddhas, at Dunhuang, originally excavated in 366 A.D. There are 492 caves still preserved, with frescoes covering*

4,500 sq. m. (50,000 sq. ft.) and more than 2,000 colored carved figures of different dynasties covering a period of 1,000 years. There are also five wooden-eaved structures of the Tang and Song dynasties. The caves form the largest treasure house of Buddhist art in China. Dunhuang is at the west end of the Gansu Corridor, and was a place of strategic importance on the old Silk Road.

217. *Five of the famous Six Steeds of the Zhau Tomb, now displayed in the Museum of the Province of Shaanxi. Originally in the tomb of the Tang emperor Tai Zhong at Li Shiming, these vivid profiles in relief were carved in 637, in memory of the six steeds ridden by the emperor during the wars that consolidated the Tang empire.*

218

219

218. *Yanan is today a thriving commercial city. In 1936 it became the home of the Central Committee of the Chinese Communist Party, and it was here that Mao Zedong, Zhou Enlai, and Zhu De directed the course of the Chinese Revolution and wrote many of their most important works. Many precious relics and sites of the Revolution are preserved in the city.*

219. *The College of Minority Nationalities in the Northwest is at the foot of Mount Wuquan (the Mountain of Springs) near Lanzhou in the province of Gansu. A comprehensive college built in 1950, it now counts among its students the members of twenty-five different ethnic groups—the Han, the Hui, the Uygur, the Hazak, and others.*

220. *The Great Mosque at Tongxin, in the Autonomous Region of Ningxia. The Hui people, who constitute 30% of the population of the region, are followers of Islam. The Great Mosque, built in the fifteenth century, is the largest in Ningxia, and a center of worship and other religious activity for the Moslems in the surrounding area.*

221

221. Camels at a watering point in the desert of Xinjiang. Enormous areas of the western provinces of China are made up of desert, where camels are just as normal a feature of the landscape as they are further south in the deserts of North Africa and the Arab countries.

222. An old Hazak in Xinjiang, playing melodies from the Hazak prairie on the dongbula, a stringed instrument of the region.

223. *Remotest China—the vast and barren scenery of the Tashikuergan Tazir Autonomous District, bounded by the Pamir Mountains.*

222

285

Chronology

B.C.	ca. 500,000	Peking Man
	ca. 4000	Yangshao culture, Henan; Banpo Village, Shaanxi
	ca. 1500	Ruins of Yin at Xiaotun, province of Henan
	early 11th c.	Changan (Xi an) capital of the Western Zhou
	1108	Building of Luoyang begun by Prince Jidan of Zhou
	770	Zhou capital moved from Changan to Luoyang
	ca. 500	Building of Suzhou begun by Wu Zixu
	551–479	Confucius
	513	Introduction of iron smelting
	ca. 400	First walls built for defense by the Warring States
	343–278	Qu Yuan, China's first major poet
	3rd c.	Magnetic compass in use
	221	Unification of China under Qin rule ends the Warring States Period
	214	Walls of Qin, Zhao, and Yan linked to form the Great Wall
	209	Death of Qin Shi Huang, first emperor of all China
	138	Zhang Qian travels to the West by route of the Silk Road
A.D.	67	Introduction of Buddhism in China
	78–139	Zhang Heng, inventor of the seismograph
	ca. 105	Invention of paper
	3rd c.	Fleet from the Kingdom of Wu reaches Taiwan
	366	Mogao caves, Dunhuang
	460–490	Yunggang grottoes
	5th c.	Longmeng grottoes
	581	Reunion of China under the Sui dynasty
	606	Introduction of a written-examination system for the selection of officials (in use to the 20th c.)
	early 7th c.	Construction of the Grand Canal
	7th c.	Invention of printing from type
	627–649	Reign of the Tang emperor Tai Zong, perhaps the highest point of Chinese ancient history
	602–664	Xuan Zhuang (journey to the Ganges and southern India)
	688–763	Jian Zhen (journey to Japan)
	713	Giant Buddha of Leshan begun
	701–762	Li Bai (Li Po), poet
	712–770	Du Fu, poet
	725	Establishment of the Han-lin Academy for training high officials
	960	Reunion of China under the Song dynasty
	10th c.	Rockets with niter powder produced
	early 11th c.	Gunpowder used for firing
	12th c.	Development of printing and porcelain
	1175	The Sleeping Buddha of Dazu begun
	1211	Beginning of Mongol invasions; devastation of North China
	1215	Beijing sacked by Genghis Khan
	1227	Death of Genghis Khan
	ca. 1210–1300	Guan Hanqing, dramatist
	1257	Kublai Khan transfers residence to Zhongdu, rebuilt as Dadu
	1268–1279	Conquest of all China by Kublai Khan
	1274–1291	Marco Polo in Dadu (Beijing)
	1294	Death of Kublai Khan
	14th c.	Wang Shifu, dramatist
	1368–1398	Mongols driven from China by the first Ming emperor
	ca. 1400	Ming capital transferred from Nanjing to Beijing
	1403–1424	The Great Wall extended and rebuilt
	1405–1433	Seven crossings of the Western Ocean to East Africa and the Red Sea by Zheng He
	15th/16th c.	Great period of Ming porcelain; development of acupuncture
	early 17th c.	Matteo Ricci in China; encouragement of Jesuit missionaries

1644	Peasant uprising under Li Zichan captures Beijing
1662–1722	Emperor Kang Xi (Qing dynasty), famous as military commander, statesman, and scholar
18th c.	Greatest territorial expansion of China
1840–1842	The Opium War; China opened to the Western world
1842	Peace of Nanking, agreeing to the cession of Hongkong and allowing trade concessions in five other harbors; the beginning of aggressive policies by the European powers in China
1851	The Taiping Rebellion and the establishment of the "heavenly kingdom"
1853	The Dagger Society uprising in Shanghai
1860	Beijing occupied by French and English troops
1864	Final suppression of the "heavenly kingdom"
1893	Birth of Mao Zedong
1895	Formation of the Tung Meng Hui Society (later the Kuomintang Party) by Sun Yat-sen
1898	Birth of Zhou Enlai
1900	The Boxer Rising, popular revolt against foreigners
1911	The Double Ten uprising in Guangdong (Canton); China proclaimed a republic, with Sun Yat-sen as president
1912	Resignation of Sun Yat-sen; presidency assumed by General Yuan Shikai (to 1916)
1916–1926	Wars of the warlords for Beijing in northern China
1919	Demonstration of Beijing students against the peace treaty with Japan and the Western powers; beginning of the May 4 Movement and the abandonment of Confucianism
1921	Formation of the Communist Party of China
1925	Death of Sun Yat-sen
1925–1927	National revolution, led by Chiang Kai-shek
1927	Break between the Communists and the Kuomintang (Chiang Kai-shek); foundation of the Red Army (later the People's Army) in opposition to the Kuomintang
1927–1936	Rule of the Kuomintang
1931	Mao Zedong elected president of the first Chinese Soviet Republic
1934–1935	The Long March of the Red Army from Jiangxi to Yanan
1937–1945	The Sino-Japanese War
1949	Proclamation of the People's Republic of China with Mao Zedong as president (October 1)
1976	Death of Mao Zedong
	Death of Zhou Enlai
	Imprisonment of the Gang of Four
	Hua Guofeng president of China